THE COMPLETE CREATIVE DIRECTOR

AF096660

BIS Publishers
Timorplein 46
1094 CC Amsterdam
The Netherlands
bis@bispublishers.com
www.bispublishers.com

ISBN 978 90 636 9871 3
Copyright © 2025 Mick Mahoney and BIS Publishers.

All rights reserved. No part of this publication
may be reproduced or transmitted in any form or
by any means, electronic or mechanical, including
photocopy, recording or any information storage
and retrieval system, without permission in writing
from the copyright owners.

Every reasonable attempt has been made
to identify owners of copyright. Any errors or
omissions brought to the publisher's attention
will be corrected in subsequent editions.

Art direction by Grant Parker
Design by Alexandre Coco
Copy-editing by Rosanna Fairhead
Proofreading by Kathy Steer
Indexing by Hilary Bird

**To Paul Weinberger and
John O'Keeffe. Thank you
for your trust and belief.
You were bigger influences
than you know.**

THE COMPLETE CREATIVE DIRECTOR

A masterclass in confident creative leadership

Mick Mahoney

BIS Publishers

Foreword.	6
Introduction.	10
How to use this book.	14
Acknowledgements.	15
Notes.	230
Index.	236

1
What does it take?
16

2
The other stuff a CD does.
36

3
Coping with the chaos.
54

4
What does everyone expect from me?
74

5
Building and running a creative department.
94

6
**Clients.
Love them
or lose them.**
116

7
**How to
master
pitching.**
136

8
**Inspiring
a creative
culture across
the agency.**
154

9
**The commercials
of creativity.**
174

10
**Adapting
to change.**
194

11
**The pros and
cons of awards.**
212

Foreword.

I've always considered George Bernard Shaw's oft-quoted epigram 'Those who can, do; those who can't, teach' to be a false dichotomy. I think Aristotle was much closer to the truth when he said: 'Those who understand, teach.' For starters, some of the greatest practitioners in history have also been great teachers; it's not mutually exclusive. Albert Einstein taught theoretical physics at three universities in three different countries. J.R.R. Tolkien was an English teacher. Marie Curie, Stephen Hawking, Noam Chomsky and J. Robert Oppenheimer also made a living in the teaching profession at some point. And no one would have a pop at their talents when it came to walking the walk.

  I have always found that having a track record or validated proof of your ability as a master practitioner is something of a prerequisite if you want to gain genuine respect from those you aspire to teach. For me, Mick is the perfect marriage of theory and practice, and that's a great thing because the world needs both. I've had the privilege of seeing Mick's dual talents up close, as his strategic partner for almost a decade. I've seen this on everything from big, established, centuries-old brands to fledgling start-ups taking their first anxious steps in comms. I've worked with him to run a company of more than 1,000 employees, and I've sat in a room with him when there were just three people and a dog (literally). In terms of clients, I've watched him advise grizzled, cynical industry veterans, but equally coax and cajole enthusiastic youngsters landing their first campaigns. I've watched him execute award-winning and till-filling work on domestic and international campaigns from massive telly to social channels that weren't even theory when he started out in the business. And I've watched him sensitively nurture placement teams on their first day, and calmly steer the most talented senior creatives towards achieving more than they thought possible.

  The world needs teachers with a deep understanding of their subject, who can help to develop the next generation with their relentlessly enthused and seductively hypnotic passion for it. But it also needs lauded, awarded, respected practitioners who don't just parrot received wisdom or marketing theory.

  A note of caution: the internet (especially LinkedIn) is full of lofty listicles and gushing bullet points passing themselves off as the quick-fix solution to creating great work or becoming a brilliant creative director. But they always lack the meaningful practical advice needed to put that theory into practice, or any understanding of the multiple factors at play to enable the promised success. They feed on anxious minds.

In my eyes, there really is no one better for any creative person to learn from than Mick. He won the Cannes Grand Prix at an age when most creatives are still dreaming of their first promotion. He went on to become one of the most awarded creatives of his generation. He was also the first CCO to feature on *Campaign* magazine's Annual List of top creative leaders in three successive agencies. He has created and overseen some of the most famous and lauded work in the world. Yet he retains a relentless interest and infectious enthusiasm for the pursuit of great ideas, and for inspiring others to join him.

There is a serious lack of material to advise ambitious and talented creatives on how to make the step from writing to managing. Or how to develop the many new skills they will need as they rise through the levels to CCO and their responsibilities multiply. Until now, there has certainly been an absence of a considered and comprehensive blueprint for how to be an effective creative director, which demonstrates an understanding of the pressures, complexity and nuance needed to succeed in this most demanding of roles. Especially one written by a recognised expert. Fortunately, we now have *The Complete Creative Director*. You'll never get to be a great creative director by reading a book. But I think you'll get to be a better and more confident one by reading *this* book. And regardless of what stage of your creative leadership career you are at, even if you're a creative who is dreaming of becoming one, this text should be your constant companion. It has much to *teach* everyone about *doing*.

Kevin Chesters.
CSO, KC Consulting

You have to learn how to be a creative director. You can't just be given a title and go, 'TA-DA! NOW YOU'RE A CREATIVE DIRECTOR.'

Nadja Lossgott
Joint CCO, AMV BBDO London

Introduction.

was not a complete creative director. I've never met anyone who is. I'm not even sure it's possible to be one. But if we know what one looks like, we can all, at least, have something to aim for. And that has got to be a good thing, right?

The reason for writing this book is that, to the best of my knowledge, no one else ever has. There are a number of books that focus on a few aspects that I cover, but there is nothing that encompasses everything you will need to be aware of. In fact, there is very little training or guidance for creative leaders in the advertising and communications industries full stop. It's ad hoc at best. There's no professional qualification or industry-recognised training programme. It's as if we no longer need help, advice or nurturing once we leave art school or finish our advertising degree courses. We're expected to pick it up along the way, to learn on the job. This works to some extent for many people – it's how I learned – but we simply can't know how many people it hasn't worked for, and how much better we could all be at the role if training were available. Given how important the role is to the advertising and communications industry, I believe it's a missed opportunity not to commit to increasing professionalism and knowledge transfer, and lowering the anxiety attached to the job. It would also make a huge difference to creative departments, agencies, clients and the industry generally to have happier, calmer and more confident CDs. The more the mechanics of being a great CD are understood, the more we can focus on the work and on nurturing talent. And that is what really matters.

For years, creative directors have guarded their secrets, nervous of giving away any advantage and worried that they will look vulnerable if they admit to not knowing something. I've experienced both of those feelings. And neither is helpful. Seeking and sharing knowledge are not weaknesses – they are strengths.

I first became a creative director twenty-five years ago, and I was clueless about what my new role entailed. My intention with this book is to share what I've learned since, informed by my experiences as a CD, ECD (Executive Creative Director) and CCO (Chief Creative Officer). These experiences enable me to offer a real-world view. It's not an idealised account of what a CD could be, nor is it sugar-coated. It's a practical how-to manual that you can refer to throughout your career.

Another creative director might write a very different book, but I'm certain that we would agree on the fundamentals that underpin the role and how to succeed in it. In fact, it has been reassuring to discover through my research for this book just how closely the best minds in the business align on what 'good' looks like when it comes to being a creative director. I hope it triggers debate and that the role and its many aspects are discussed more openly than they are right now. I genuinely hope that future editions of this book contain myriad amendments and builds from all the brilliant and committed creative directors that come into contact with it. And I hope it becomes the catalyst for more support and knowledge transfer for what is an increasingly demanding and complex role.

Looking at the contents page, you might wonder why there isn't a chapter dedicated to creative leadership. It's a deliberate omission. Great creative leadership is the sum of all the sections in all the chapters of this book. It manifests itself in everyday ways, not in grand gestures. And, since this is a practical manual, I wanted to keep it that way. You will learn to lead with confidence in your own abilities, care and compassion for others, and a commitment to great work.

I wish I could say that I lived up to every point in every chapter. But I didn't. Most of the time I simply didn't know what I didn't know. There was no framework to refer to, no instruction manual, and that resulted in a lot of unhealthy anxiety and unnecessary underperformance. I would often say jokingly that I was making it up as I went along. But I really was. All creative directors are at every stage. I hope that will now start to change.

The Complete Creative Director provides clear, practical actions for you to incorporate into your working day. It will help you to become more aware of and knowledgeable about what is expected of you as a creative leader, and what is to come. You will have a clearer understanding of best practice and feel confident to tailor what you have learned to suit your unique personality. You will also have mechanisms for keeping your anxiety in check, enabling you to approach the role with greater focus and authority. You will gain a better understanding of how to build strong key relationships, both internally and externally, and how to radiate a creative culture across the business. You will be more resilient in the face of setbacks and adaptable to constant change. All this will give you more time and energy for what ultimately matters: developing great creative work.

This book covers how to create the conditions, relationships and environment to get to great work. It doesn't deal with what great work looks like. That's up to you. (And there are countless books, courses, podcasts and so on for that.)

I'm very grateful for the life that being an advertising CD/ECD/CCO has enabled me to enjoy, and I'm excited to be able to pass on what I've learned. It's an incredible rollercoaster of a career choice. And one that I've never regretted for a moment.

How to use this book.

The Complete Creative Director is not intended to be read sequentially. Feel free to do that, but it was written as a reference book, something useful to return to again and again when the need arises.

Certain topics will be more relevant to you at different stages of your creative leadership career. But there are such blurred lines and overlaps between the various creative titles and responsibilities associated with them in different agencies and organisations that it would be impossible to separate them all in a meaningful way. So I have used the term 'creative director' in its generic sense of a creative professional with leadership responsibilities. You can then determine what is relevant to you.

At the end of the book there are six blank pages for you to add your thoughts, experiences and builds so that you can personalise your copy. If you think your notes contain something I should have included, or if you have a great build on anything I've mentioned, take a photo or scan of them and send them to me at mick@mcreativeindustries.com. I plan to update the book regularly to keep it as relevant as possible.

I am also conscious that there is only so much information that you can put into a book before it becomes overwhelming and defeats its original purpose of being helpful. Fortunately, I can go into more practical detail in the *Complete Creative Director* masterclass training programme I run, or in my one-on-one coaching sessions.

Acknowledgements.

The Complete Creative Director would not have been possible without the wisdom and support given by some of the creative industry's finest minds. More than 40 hours of recorded interviews and more than 2,000 pages of transcribed notes have helped me to shape what you are about to read.

Helen Andrews – CEO, Johannes Leonardo NY
Lynsey Atkin – former CCO, McCann London
Claire Beale – Editor, Creative Salon
Chris Beresford-Hill – Global CCO, BBDO
Richard Brim – former CCO, Adam & Eve DDB London
Rob Campbell – CSO, Colenso NZ
Kevin Chesters – CSO, KC Consulting
Scott Dungate – CCO, Uncommon London
Charlie Gatsky Sinclair – President Brands & Entertainment, Uncommon
Alex Grieve – Global & London CCO, BBH
Bronwen Hemming – FD, Wieden + Kennedy London
Nicholas Hulley – Joint CCO, AMV BBDO London
Tanya Livesey – Global MD Creative & Design, TTB
Nadja Lossgott – Joint CCO, AMV BBDO London
Katie Mackay-Sinclair – Partner, Mother London
Felix Richter – CCO, Mother London
Charlie Rudd – CEO, Creative Practice, Publicis Groupe UK
Bill Scott – CEO, Droga5 London
Rodrigo Sobral – Global CCO, Oliver
David Spencer – CFO, Goodby Silverstein & Partners SF

1

What does it take?

Most creatives want to be a creative director. I did. From about two or three years into the industry, I just wanted to approve my own work. I thought I knew everything I needed to know, and that creative directors just got in the way. They were old and out of date. Looking back, they were probably only in their late thirties, but when you're twenty-three that is unimaginably ancient. It seemed to me that they were more interested in their own ideas, rarely said anything helpful, constantly tried to micromanage me, and always thought they were the smartest (and funniest) people in the room.

And then I met a good one. Very quickly I realised that a talented creative director had the ability to make me a lot better, challenge me in the right ways, elevate my work past anything I had thought possible, and make me feel there was nothing I couldn't do. I learned as much as I could from him: how he reviewed creative work, how he treated people, how he presented. (He was actually a terrible presenter, but clients loved him for it. More on that later.) I went on to do the same thing with every good creative director I came across. I also learned a great deal about what not to do from some terrible creative directors.

Creatives want to be a creative director for a number of reasons. Money. Title. Influence. Control. Nurture. Vision. Whatever the reason (and I don't think it's significant why you first decide it's for you), all that matters is that you want to be a good one. A good one will lift everyone around them to achieve more, learn more and enjoy more. In truth, it's not hard to be a creative director, it's just really hard to be a good one.

Now, the fact that you're reading this and considering the question is a good sign. You're obviously keen to get it right, and you recognise that you never stop learning. Realistically, very few people have all the attributes of a great creative director. Most have more of some and less of others. And that's OK – don't beat yourself up. But it is important that you're as aware of your weaknesses as you are of your strengths, and that you work on them or compensate for them. It's also crucial that you don't try to turn yourself into something you're not. Over time, that will make you very unhappy.

Very few people ever give much thought to what skills are needed for the role. People recruiting for it rarely look past the work you've made, awards you've won and agencies you've worked in. They want a good PR headline to draw attention to their agency, but they don't drill down into what really matters. I don't remember ever being asked about my approach to nurturing young talent, for example. And people seeking the role rarely consider if it's a good fit for their skill set. They're blinded by the cachet and the pay rise. Quite often, people are simply elevated into the role at their existing agency because the agency wants to keep them and it's a recognised promotion. That's how I first became a creative director.

I hope this chapter will give potential creative directors – and the industry more generally – a clearer framework with which to make an informed assessment. It should also help creative directors who are already in roles to spot the gaps in their game. If you're able to read through the next ten sections and recognise yourself in at least two-thirds of them, there's a good chance that you're in the right job and will do well. But if you don't, my advice is to take another path. Being a creative director is not for the faint-hearted and it takes a great deal more than being a brilliant creative. If you don't have the skills or aren't willing to commit to developing them, you're in for a tough time. So, what does it take?

Being a creative is like playing draughts or checkers. Then, when you become a creative director, you have to LEARN TO PLAY CHESS.

Felix Richter
CCO, Mother London

Lots of great creatives end up in creative leadership roles when they'd be way better off staying as great creatives. In fact, there are lots of people in every discipline who were **GREAT PRACTITIONERS BUT ENDED UP AS BAD LEADERS.** That the industry seems to value 'title' over 'standards' is one of our great short-sighted tragedies.

Rob Campbell
CSO, Colenso NZ

Be honest with yourself.

What makes you happy at work? The more you enjoy what you're doing, the harder you apply yourself and the more successful you will inevitably be. But this is a question that you must be completely honest with yourself about. If it's spending your days quietly solving creative briefs with your partner, focusing solely on creative output, losing yourself down creative rabbit holes and delighting in the craft of production, being a creative director might not make you happy. And you being a creative director would be unlikely to make anyone else happy, either, because your focus won't be where it needs to be. There will still be snippets of that, depending on the particular demands of your creative leadership role, but it won't be how you'll spend your day. Instead, there will be more meetings, more interruptions, more diverse draws on your time, all in the pursuit of creating an environment that allows other people to create great work.

If you're not ready for that shift but can see a time when you will be, stick with it for now; there's no rush to be a creative director. The best ones tend to have plenty of work under their belts. You also don't have to become a creative director to make progress in your career. This is one of the biggest misconceptions in the industry. If you just want to write and make great ads, do it. Every creative director is desperate for talented people in their department who are brilliant at doing that. And if you can be relied on to deliver, you'll always be in great demand. So, stop reading this book, get back to what you love, and put your heart and soul into being brilliant at it. You might even find that your future lies in being the Head of Art or Head of Copy, or perhaps even directing or screenwriting. Realistically, you might not earn as much as a creative director, but you will be happier and more fulfilled.

Temperament.

This is the biggest single differentiator between success and failure. As a creative – if you're good enough – you can be as outspoken and contrary as you like. I'm not advocating that, but you're in a tolerant and liberal environment that makes allowances for unpredictable behaviour and encourages rebellion if it leads to brilliant outcomes. But as a creative director onwards you'll have to be more considered. Don't interpret that as dull. You should still be challenging and disruptive to the status quo, but just be aware that you no longer live in such an accommodating, understanding world.

You must be able to reassure a broad range of people that you can be relied on to deliver when the pressure is on. That you can be responsible. Can you take a breath before you disagree with a different point of view from your own? Can you keep your emotions in check when a junior client, with a full eighteen months of experience, explains to you why your idea doesn't work and what to do to make it better? Can you hold your nerve when all around are questioning you? Do you feel confronted by feedback? Are your hackles rising just reading this?

If you're easily triggered or find it hard to keep your emotions in check, you will struggle, since there is no shortage of potential flashpoints in a creative director's average day. No one wants to deal with someone who constantly overreacts. Your passion for great work must show itself in positive ways that inspire others and act as a beacon of creativity, not by storming off and sulking like a spoiled child. Everyone will be looking to you to find a way forwards. It's a big responsibility. The more you can reassure colleagues and clients that you have it under control, the better.

Emotional intelligence.

As a rule, creative people are emotionally adaptable and empathetic, and these are great skills for a creative director to have. Being able to read a room and adjust your approach will be fundamental to your success. As a creative, you can be all 'This is me, take it or leave it,' but as a creative director you will need to flex your tone and energy constantly to match the ever-changing needs of others. The days of the gruff, moody creative director who expected everyone to bow to his or her will are thankfully long gone. And so are the people who were willing to enable them. That won't be tolerated.

    The success of a pitch, meeting or creative review will depend on you having the emotional intelligence to know what energy, what version of yourself you are required to bring to it, and that you will almost certainly be the most influential factor in that success. By the time I became a CCO I was having between ten and fifteen meetings a day: interviewing a nervous young team, holding a client presentation, a creative review for a pitch, a pre-production meeting with a highly strung director and nervous client, a finance meeting to discuss cutbacks being demanded by global, an edit, management prep for an all-agency meeting, and so on. Approaching them all in the same way would have been disastrous. You have to be able to plan ahead, triage the mood of the room, and act so as to get the result you need. You can't expect everyone to fit around you. You also can't carry over your frustration from one meeting to another. That makes you appear unpredictable and unprofessional.

    It takes a great deal of self-awareness to know how much you're affecting someone's day. And a great deal of determination to affect it only positively.

A giver, not a taker.

Another common misconception is that the creative director gets the pick of the briefs. Yes, in theory, you could decide that that's how you want to play it, but don't expect anyone good to want to work for you, or that you'll have an energised culture in your department.

In reality, you will mostly have to pick up the difficult briefs that can suck the life out of a department, or the last-minute ones that haven't been cracked. (Unless, of course, you are a creative director in a very small, overstretched department; then you just do whatever needs doing.) You must also be willing to give away your best thinking to help teams from time to time, and never take credit for it. You'll even have to applaud as they walk up to the stage to collect an award for it, without mumbling that it was actually your idea. You must be willing to give without expecting anything back. The return on your investment is to earn the trust and respect of your department, and their belief that your words and actions are for the right reasons, not to promote your own interests.

I once had to tell an ECD who worked for me that I didn't think he was cut out for the role. Teams kept trying to bypass him. Account teams never asked for him on accounts or pitches. He regularly wrote on the best briefs and constantly prioritised his own ideas. As a result, no one trusted that his opinions weren't simply self-serving. He replied, 'I can't stop being an ECD – I'd miss the power.' I was lost for words momentarily. 'What power?' was my eventual reply. There *is* no power, only responsibility. He saw it differently and decided to move on to be an ECD elsewhere. Sadly for him, he stuck with his approach, and predictably his career took a nosedive. No one wants to work for a creative director who puts themselves first.

There's a mind shift that has to happen when you go from a doer to a leader. As a copywriter or art director the work you produce is your accruing value in the industry, in the company and with the clients you work with. So, by hook or by crook, you've got to keep adding to the body of work by doing work that makes you stand out. In the switch to being a fully fledged creative director or a young chief creative officer, you have to understand that **OTHER PEOPLE'S SUCCESS IS YOUR ONLY SUCCESS.**

Chris Beresford-Hill
Global CCO, BBDO

You have to ensure that it doesn't come with any sense of arrogance, but you do have to **BACK YOURSELF** and have the inner confidence that you know what you're doing and that when you make a decision, you think it's going to be helpful and move the project forward.

Alex Grieve
Global & London CCO, BBH

Confident in your own decisions.

People-pleasers need not apply. It's impossible to keep everyone happy. Trying to do so will also make it impossible for you to do your job successfully. If the work is provocative, single-minded and different, it will attract points of view that might not agree with yours. Everyone looks at work from a different vantage point, depending on what they are held responsible for. Hear them out; they may have a valid point. But remember, your responsibility is to create famous and effective work. So you'll need to be able to stand your ground. You'll hear every reason under the sun why a piece of work can't be the way you believe it should be, so you must be sure of yourself.

You'll need to be unreasonable from time to time. Being unreasonable doesn't mean being rude or unpleasant, however. It means steadfastly sticking to your views, with good reason, when it would be much easier to agree with someone. People will be looking to you for guidance and confidence, and if you're unsure of yourself, it ripples out in a heartbeat. This is genuinely hard day in, day out, because rarely will you be in possession of all the answers or able to be certain of the outcomes. Creative work is not a fact. You will be relying on your intuition and judgement. But if you find yourself agreeing for the sake of an easy life, you're done for. It may be a short-term win, but it will bring a long-term loss of trust and respect.

The role is also made much harder if you approach it combatively. Confrontation never works out for anyone. You may well end up winning the argument, but hostility is harboured and it will come back to bite you another day. This also sets the tone for an unhealthy culture. If people feel they can't disagree with you without getting shouted down, you'll end up surrounded by people with no opinions.

Nurturing.

I'm not convinced that this comes naturally to many creatives in the early stages of their leadership careers. And that is hardly surprising. To achieve creative recognition is hard. The competition is fierce, and to succeed – whether through famous work or awards or both – demands single-minded, selfish determination. To be expected suddenly to switch to nurturing others takes some adjustment, and not everyone can find it in themselves to do it.

This is one of the biggest responsibilities of the role. But it's also one of the most satisfying. Being the person who creates an environment in which others can succeed is addictive, and ultimately far more rewarding than your own individual success. However, it takes a certain kind of person to want to do it and to get genuine pleasure from it.

Are you pleased when others succeed? Are you the first person to say 'well done' – and mean it? Are you genuinely interested in people? In their welfare, their lives, their backgrounds, their interests? Or their careers? If not, no matter how talented you are, people won't follow you. Leadership is all about gaining followers. Any creative worth their salt will only follow a creative director who nurtures them. They know that if you don't, their chances of success are dramatically reduced.

The ability to nurture great talent in a high-pressure environment is often a measure of how confident a creative director feels in their position and their ability to do their job well. It's hard to nurture if you yourself feel threatened, and it takes a real leader to prioritise nurturing when no one is nurturing them. But if you can do this, you will build a loyal and supportive department around you, who recognise your value and want to deliver for you.

All of us have been in a relationship where it feels one-sided, where the person you're dating has it all on their terms. They're always late, they put you down a bit, they don't make you feel good about yourself. And then you break up with them and you meet someone who cares about your day, who makes you feel really good about yourself, who stretches you, challenges you, and they **SEE SOMETHING IN YOU THAT YOU NEVER SAW IN YOURSELF**, and they make you feel amazing. That's what the creative director's job is.

**Katie Mackay-Sinclair
Partner, Mother London**

Impossibly high standards.

Are you willing to drive yourself and everyone else around you, including your friends and family, nuts with your need to make the work better? To lose sleep and never settle until it's excellent, even when no one has asked you to, or thanks you for it? Great creative directors are. They are their own toughest critics, and no one drives them harder than they drive themselves. And that is table stakes to be successful. You can, of course, adopt a far more laissez-faire approach, but don't expect to be in high demand, because first and foremost, the creative director will always be judged on the work the agency produces, not on how easy-going they are.

You will be faced with countless perfectly reasonable requests to make changes to work that will affect the quality. These will annoy and frustrate you for what you perceive to be others' lack of commitment to great work. But you must also be able to find the time to explain why that reasonable ask will affect the work, and not just shout in frustration.

It's also worth being aware that if you are this person, you will need to know when *not* to be this person. You can't take every brief to the ends of the Earth in pursuit of perfection. That burns through profit margins that you should want to protect for more deserving projects, and it will also demotivate your team. Some briefs or clients will never be worth the time or effort. (More on this in Chapter 6.)

You will also need to understand that you can't drive everyone around you as hard as you drive yourself. This can be frustrating when you're under pressure, but not everyone is like you or wants to be like you, nor should you expect them to be. You're in this role because you're driven. Your high standards must be a beacon that draws people to want to emulate them, not a stick to beat them with.

Strategic and creative.

Creatives think about executions, whereas creative directors must think about executions that build brands. You can only do that by understanding brand strategy. How does what you're doing inform or influence the ecosystem that exists around your brand? The complexity of how brands communicate now demands a strategic consistency across multiple touchpoints, in many cases even more than creative consistency. And, as guardian of the brand, you will be expected to have an informed view on how this is achieved. I've always wanted to understand the audience, the media thinking, the business and category context, and so on – anything to give me a broader view of the brand I'm creative directing and what I can do to influence it.

If you are to create work with real meaning and emotional resonance, you must also have a deep interest in people, the world they live in and what motivates them. In my experience, this empathy comes naturally to most creative people, but you can never know too much about your audience. Understanding them and their needs is often the key to solving the problem. The best creative directors could just as easily have been planners. They are as interested in solving the problem strategically as they are creatively, and they see the two things as indivisible. They also really enjoy having a strategic partner to work with, sharing a vision of what they want to achieve.

Get involved in the brief, don't wait for it to arrive on your desk. Good strats will love you for it. If strategy sends you to sleep, however, and you just want a good brief to execute, you will find it hard to oversee work that builds the brand. This will also mean that you are allowing the strategic responsibility to fall to someone else, which will weaken your ability to sell or defend the creative work.

Relentlessness.

Truth is, there are generally more downs than ups in this industry. Perhaps it's more accurate to say that there are more challenges than resolutions. Success in the role often depends on you being able to keep coming back for more, undaunted and unbowed, your commitment and energy levels as high as ever. In fact, this is true of most leadership roles in the creative industries, since there isn't a linear path to finding answers. Creativity is impossible to control or industrialise; it's unique and bespoke every time, and that makes it difficult to manage.

Can you dust yourself down after a knockback? Can you keep going with a smile on your face? Can you find time for others when you have no time for yourself? Being a CD is not a job, it's a lifestyle choice. It will find a way into every moment of your life. There will never be a time when you don't have something preying on your mind. All this means you must be able to keep pushing yourself long after everyone else has stopped.

One of my old CSO (Chief Strategic Officer) partners with a particularly sardonic sense of humour kept four Weebles (Google it) on his desk. When things got more difficult than usual, he would flick them with his fingers so that they wobbled, while singing the jingle for them – 'Weebles wobble but they don't fall down' – and laughing quietly to himself.

I discuss coping strategies for keeping yourself equal to the task in Chapter 3. You will need them. Becoming overwhelmed by the constant pressure of the job is avoidable and will enable you to see that pressure as a privilege and not a problem. Almost always, the pressure is presenting an opportunity, and you have to be in the right frame of mind to grasp it.

If you're in a creative leadership role, you need to love what you do, because YOU NEVER REALLY SWITCH OFF. There is always a weight there of some kind of problem that isn't quite solved.

Alex Grieve
Global & London CCO, BBH

Because of the number of hats you need to wear as a creative leader, the SPHERE OF INFLUENCE that you have to create, whether that's your clients, journalists, colleagues and so on, you have to have good communication skills, and an ability to relate to people.

Tanya Livesey
Global MD Creative & Design, TTB

Great communicator.

Ironically, this is something that many creative directors fall down on. It's quite possible that the first ten years of your career have been spent mostly talking to your creative partner. You've almost certainly said on more than one occasion that you would rather your work did the talking for you. There's also a very good chance that you are introverted. (Introversion is quite common among creatives.) But now that you are a creative director, if you're not spending a good part of your day in conversation, you aren't doing it right. Talk to your teams. Ask them how they are. Tell them your plans. Talk to the planners. Ask them how they are … etc. This doesn't mean that you have to be garrulous or extroverted. Being a good communicator doesn't mean that you must do all the talking – it often means that you do all the listening – but it does mean that you don't shut yourself away from everyone and keep your thoughts to yourself. Take some time at the beginning or end of meetings to engage with people outside the immediate context of the meeting.

Everyone in the agency is interested to know what you are thinking. No one impacts their day more than you. They will feed off your thoughts, which help them to map what success looks like for them. It's important that you realise just how important you are as a source of information. A few well-chosen words of encouragement, an inspiring speech or an impromptu talk will go a very long way towards creating confidence and momentum in the agency.

It's also important that you are willing to share your thoughts and observations more publicly, in order to champion yourself, your business and your clients. This is a great way to attract talent and new business.

2
The other stuff a CD does.

Getting to great work is your priority. No question. You can be the loveliest and most popular person in the agency, but if the work isn't good enough you won't last long in the role. 'You're only as good as your last ad' is a common industry adage, and although you have more leeway than being judged on your last ad, it's not a million miles from the truth. Building and running a creative department and overseeing the creative output will naturally be the most significant draw on your time, and consequently these have their own chapter (Chapter 5).

When I first became a creative director leading an agency, I was blissfully unaware that my responsibilities extended beyond delivering great work, or that anything else even really mattered. I was utterly focused on output. I assumed that if I concentrated on developing the work, it would be someone else's responsibility to do everything else. And by 'everything else' I meant everything I didn't know anything about. I didn't know what I didn't know. As a creative, your perspective is fairly restricted and you're rarely aware of the other moving parts that a creative director must be cognisant of and involved in if the team is to stand a chance of producing consistently brilliant work. From operations to training, from agency creds to culture – everything that means you have access to and good relationships with great accounts, brilliant, motivated creatives, a silky and productive process, an inspiring culture, a strong new business pipeline, and a bunch of other things that create the conditions and environment for great work to happen. All roads lead to the work.

I eventually learned what else needed my attention, and how it was all interrelated. This chapter is dedicated to explaining those demands on your time that you might be less familiar with. Many of the points will not feel as relevant in the early stages of your creative leadership career as they will when you're a creative director in charge of a department. However, it's important to be aware of and prepared for the next stage of your leadership career; this is a great way to make the transition easier, to understand how you can support your CCO, and even to demonstrate to the agency that you are ready for a bigger role. It's also never too soon to start developing the skills and the thinking you will need.

Preparation is fundamental to success. The runway for creative directors to learn the role is becoming shorter and shorter, so you can no longer afford to wait until you get the role to discover what's required. The points in this chapter must feel familiar before you start.

As much as anything, this chapter is about opening your eyes to the responsibilities of a creative leader of an agency, not just of a creative department, or even of an account. To take a wider view of the world you are in – a world that will in time mean you taking responsibility for certain aspects of the business that don't interest you. These may not grip you as much as the creative work, but they are just as important for you to drive or to have a clear view on.

It's probably the most POLYMATH, all-encompassing role in an agency.

Bill Scott
CEO, Droga5 London

Leadership team management.

You've spent most of your career in a creative team; it's been you two against the world. Now you're part of a team that contains a planner, an account person and a production lead. How that team bonds and works together will determine the success of your agency. A dysfunctional management team will bring it down in a heartbeat.

This principle is no different if you are running an account. In fact, you should look upon your account leadership team as a training ground. It offers an excellent opportunity to develop your approach without the same level of scrutiny or pressure, and it's a great way to develop relationships with other future agency leaders who might want to work with you again one day. It's essential that you commit time to clarifying individual responsibilities, as well as shared beliefs, shared principles and a way of working together. Hopefully, through this process you will find common ground and a collective view of what success looks like, but don't stop working on it.

You can never be too clear on each other's thoughts and plans, never be too united. That takes time, trust and commitment. If there are any gaps between you, they will widen in the maelstrom of your working day, so you must be able to talk through differences in a constructive and respectful way. You have to want each other to win. There will also be numerous occasions when you need your partners' support and backing. It may sound like a cliché, but it's lonely running a business (and an account), and there will be times when the only people who really understand the pressure you're under or who can help you are your leadership partners. The knowledge that they have your back will get you through most situations. And never forget that you only get back what you put in.

Agency positioning.

What does your agency stand for? What makes it different from other agencies? Why should clients want to work with you? Why should the best talent want to join you? What are your key strengths? What type of work do you do?

You must have an opinion on all these things and agree them all with your leadership team. Then turn them into your agency positioning, website and creds. This will allow everyone who works with you or is considering working with you – whether as a client or an employee – to be clear what you're all about, and what exactly success looks like to you. It doesn't have to be complicated or intellectual, but it must be clear and engaging.

We do this for our clients' brands every day, yet we rarely give it the focus it deserves when it's for our own agency. You would be amazed by how few agencies have a clear and memorable positioning that distinguishes them. In general, they are a sea-of-same, dull, overlong, self-indulgent, rational and frequently banging on about the efficiency of their process. That's like a restaurant selling itself on how clean its kitchen is, instead of how incredible the food is. And it's the exact opposite of what we tell clients to do. They rarely have a creative focus or point of view, which attests to the fact that very few creative directors take responsibility for them. It's no coincidence that the best, most successful examples of agency positioning belong to agencies with very strong creative identities. Make sure yours is one of those.

The single biggest driver of agency choice by potential clients and employees is the work you produce and your creative culture. So, in agency positioning your voice matters. You will bring emotion to it, and that alone will elevate it above most other agency positionings and creds.

Project management.

Project management is not your day-to-day responsibility, but who runs it and how it runs is. 'Head of Project Management' can be a key role in your team. You must be able to trust that they and their team will deliver for you. No one has more contact with creatives than project management, so the experience has to be a good one. Weed out the moaners; you need can-do dynamos that keep enthusiasm and energy levels high.

Consider how you want reviews to be arranged and brief your HOPM to arrange them accordingly. Some creative directors like to review with all teams at once, others with teams individually. Some like to include the planners in the reviews, or even the account team. Everyone has their own approach – there's no right or wrong. But if your HOPM is clear about your preferences, they can put all the right people in the room at the right time, knowing what you are expecting from them. In a fast-moving, deadline-driven environment, this ensures momentum and focus. PMs (project managers) are also the masters of pulling presentations and pitches into shape. Make sure they are clear about your expectations and they will almost always take great pleasure in exceeding them.

Because PMs spend their days talking to everyone across the agency, they are good barometers of mood. They pride themselves on being the first to know what's going on in the agency, and they will keep you up to date with any mounting tension, personal problems, etc., so that you can deal with them accordingly.

Great project management enables the smooth running and successful deployment of your department. PMs are always the most proactive, collaborative people in the agency. And if they aren't, replace them. Because they should be.

Production.

No one can affect the execution of the work more than production, so it's important to make sure they understand your idea of 'good'. Producers, whether for moving image, stills or any other form of creative content, are an extension of the creative department. Their role isn't to shepherd errant creatives into cabs; it's to bring their knowledge and passion for their craft to bear on a creative project. To use them in any other way is a missed opportunity. Treat your Head of Production (titles vary by agency) as a creative partner. They are smart, creative people motivated by craft to create great work. They will be aware of current and emerging talent and trends, and have a lot to bring to the creative process. The more respected and valued they feel by you and your department, the more they will give.

A good creative producer can also help to alleviate the pressure on you during the production process. Most are excellent communicators who can make sure everyone necessary feels updated and consulted. They understand that assumptions and unchecked details can lead to costly mistakes, and they are nature's triple-checkers. By over-communicating, they eliminate ambiguity, minimise the potential for error, and ensure that every project runs like clockwork. This goes a long way towards keeping client's and production company's trust and enthusiasm in a project.

So, hold them close. Invest time in seeking out their opinions. I was fortunate to have one of the very best production partners throughout two of my CCO jobs, and she never failed to make it look as though I had it all effortlessly under control, regardless of whether I did or not.

New business leads.

It took a while for me to realise that chasing new business was anything to do with me. Most agencies have a dedicated new-business person, and I don't recommend that you replace them with you, since they will be busy doing lots of things that you don't want to do and frankly wouldn't be very good at. But I do recommend that you reach out to ex-clients, or clients of accounts that you are interested in. There is no one more compelling or persuasive to a client than a creative director who is excited about their account. Smart clients know that their fate often lies in the emotional connection a creative director feels for their brand.

I wouldn't be surprised if experienced creative directors reading this are thinking: 'What?! I'm not doing that!' But it pays to develop an antenna for new business. It needn't take up much time, perhaps an hour or so a week. It could involve emailing to congratulate a former client who has moved jobs or been promoted. Or getting in touch to tell them that you've just done some incredible work that you'd love to show them because you think it might be relevant to them. You could follow them on LinkedIn and comment positively on their posts. Our job is to find brilliant ways to sell things, so find a brilliant way to sell yourself and your agency. Your position will also be strengthened if you are the one who holds the client relationship, and that's never a bad thing.

You will get lots of knock-backs, but don't be discouraged. Persistence pays off. When it's time for them to look for a new agency, you've increased your chance of getting on to the pitch list. It's amazing how frequently clients change jobs or call pitches, so think of it as a long-term project. I've worked with numerous clients on many occasions when they are working for a different brand and I'm at a different agency. All it takes is bothering to stay in touch.

Client relationships.

It's never too early to start developing your own relationships with clients. The better your relationships are, the better your chances of getting great work out, keeping accounts and winning new ones. Developing a client relationship is not someone else's responsibility, it's yours. Not the day-to-day stuff of chasing invoices or setting up meetings – that must never fall to you – but your responsibility is to become a trusted partner whom clients want to turn to when they need advice or have a concern or problem. Knowing that they have that relationship with you will mean a lot to them.

Yes, it can be invasive at times, particularly when they want to talk outside work hours, but it's always worth it. Look at it the other way round. If there was someone who had the power to fix your problem, wouldn't you appreciate them taking your call when you were in a tight spot? The role of a CMO (Chief Marketing Officer) is extremely difficult, and they need trusted partners. With that trust comes a great opportunity to do good work together. No one ever willingly took a risk on work with someone they didn't like or trust. So give them your mobile number and tell them to call whenever they need you. Don't hide behind the business lead.

This is another topic that matters enough to have its own chapter (Chapter 6). Getting to know your clients as people takes time and effort. They are looking to you for reassurance that they are with the right agency. Doing great work for them should be your primary objective, but never lose sight of how you get to it. Make sure you've built bridges in the process, not burned them. If you're running the department, you have the added responsibility of seeing that the right balance of people represents the agency on an account. The creative lead needs to be heard, but equally must not dominate the team or be deaf to the needs of the client. It's up to you to set the boundaries.

Industry PR.

This is not mandatory. No one will fire you for not doing it.
I was reluctant to do it for a long time because I felt uncomfortable drawing public attention to myself. But over time I realised that it made a big difference to new business, agency awareness and our profile. If you're in an agency that needs help boosting its profile, which is 99% of the industry, it really helps.

If you have the opportunity to work with an industry PR person, take it. They will be able to point you in the right direction in terms of topics and platforms. If you struggle to get something published, use your own media channels. Work on building your LinkedIn and Instagram channels.

You might want to write opinion pieces on the future of commercial creativity, or give a view on the impact of AI on creative development. It's important to realise that people want to know what you think. You're an opinion leader in the industry now. If you're not comfortable pronouncing on broader topics, restrict your PR to talking about the work your agency is producing. Perhaps give a journalist an exclusive 'making of' story, or offer an opinion on the latest industry talking point. You're not selling out; you're selling your agency. Work out what you are confident talking about and plan for the next three months to get exposure for it.

Awards are great PR for yourself and your agency. Not just winning them, but judging them. Often, the higher your profile the better your chances are of being asked to be involved.

Don't worry if PR doesn't come naturally – it rarely does. But it is incredibly valuable in helping you stand out in a very crowded marketplace. The reality is that few people will know what you're doing if you don't tell them.

Profile is massive. Because that's what people are buying into. There's a model called the THEORY OF PIE, developed by Harvey Coleman. Pie is Performance, Image and Exposure.

PERFORMANCE – your work, what you do – is only worth 10% of your likely success.

IMAGE – your brand – is worth 30%.

EXPOSURE – your network, how you're seen, how you're out there, your profile – is 60% of your ability to be successful.

Let's be honest, there's quite a lot of 'Emperor's New Clothes' out there that are getting awards. And the reason a lot of that work gets the kudos it does is because the figureheads in those agencies are extremely good at PR.

Tanya Livesey
Global MD Creative & Design, TTB

There's so much pressure in the business, and sometimes it can be joyless. It's crushing when we lose a pitch, or when a production you think is going to go ahead is cancelled. **NEVER UNDERESTIMATE HOW FRAGILE TALENT CAN BE.** You've got to be visible, and vocal, you've got to almost exaggerate your parental nurturing. I think this is true now more than ever, because it's tough out there.

Bill Scott
CEO, Droga5 London

Pastoral care.

Agencies are not factories with workers clocking on and off. They are human capital businesses, which means the only real value they have is the people who come in to work every day. So, you need to invest time and money in making sure they are in great shape physically and mentally so that they can be their best selves. Unless they feel positively engaged and happy, you can't expect them to go above and beyond for you.

It's down to you and your leadership team to agree how you are going to support people's needs. How will you ensure that employees with disabilities are seen and heard? How long should holiday entitlements be? What kind of bonuses will you award? Should everyone have equal medical cover? And so on and so on. These are all things that create positive working environments and make people feel rewarded for their hard work. Everyone who works for you should expect to feel trusted and respected. Hopefully this will come to you naturally, but if it doesn't, don't panic – just be aware that it doesn't and work on cultivating it. Showing an interest in the people around you even when you're under pressure goes a long way towards building respect and trust. Everyone wants to feel seen by you; it's one of your biggest responsibilities.

It's also becoming progressively more important as we are more tech-connected that you demonstrate your understanding of the separation between work and home life. Respect their right to have a cut-off point and trust them to do their job, and you will be rewarded.

Consider your policy on training and development, too. Training is one of the biggest reasons for employee retention, as it demonstrates your willingness to develop people's skills and careers. And it's often far cheaper than having to find replacements.

Culture.

There's no point looking at anyone else. You are now the living, breathing embodiment of the agency's culture, whether you like it or not. Your actions signal what you consider to be acceptable. If you're a shouter, then shouting at people is OK. You now have a culture in which the loudest shouters prosper. If you're a big lunchtime drinker, guess what? You'll never be stuck for drinking buddies. It will result in a fun, sociable culture, but probably not the most productive or dynamic. Your behaviours will be amplified. You set the standards and the rules.

So think carefully about what you want the culture to be. It's easy to declare 'hardworking, supportive, fun' on the wall in big, vibrant vinyls or pink neon, and say that's what your agency culture is, but if that's not how you and the leadership team behave, it will never be your culture. In truth, there are many agencies that define their culture in this way, using aspirational words that are rarely backed by actions. This is counterproductive because it makes the leadership team look as though they lack self-awareness and, worse still, are out of touch with the way people really feel about working for them. The only cultures that prosper are those born out of truth. If you foster and reward curiosity and the agency recognises that, curiosity can be one of your values. But if the reality is that you just want people to do what you tell them, you're setting your culture up to fail and breeding discontent.

Figure out what will help you do the best work in the most inclusive way, make sure that these are real and achievable ambitions, enshrine them as the constituent parts of your culture through clear, communicated actions, embody them personally, then encourage everyone else to live up to them too. Creating a strong, credible culture isn't complicated, but it does take a great deal of passion and principle.

Culture isn't DRINKS ON A FRIDAY and a pool table. Culture is your expectation of people.

Kevin Chesters
CSO, KC Consulting

We work in an industry that's as SHITTY or as GREAT as we want it to be.

Richard Brim
Former CCO, Adam & Eve DDB London

Politics.

This depends on where you work, of course. But most creative businesses are prone to some degree of political manoeuvring. About a third of office workers cite politics as a major factor in feelings of unhappiness at work. This figure rises the larger the company gets, to as much as 85% in companies with more than 1,000 employees. So it's important that you deal with it, and don't turn a blind eye because it's not your problem. It *is* your problem. It affects morale, collaboration, staff turnover and performance, and it will undermine your efforts to build a positive creative culture.

Office politics are driven by all kinds of things, but jealousy and insecurity are the most common in creative departments. We've all experienced those feelings and we know how much they can affect behaviour and mood.

Creative directors typically don't have any training or experience in conflict resolution, so I recommend that you seek advice from the human resources department if you have one, or from some other source. This is a difficult space to navigate successfully without training, so avoid steaming in, even with everyone's best interests at heart. Stay calm, seek help, and harmony will be restored much more quickly.

It's also worth reflecting on your own behaviour. Politics tend to be a manifestation of culture or the way you are making people feel. This comes back to self-awareness and emotional intelligence. Are you inadvertently contributing to the situation? Are you being open and transparent about future plans? Are you being supportive of people who are under pressure? Are you pitting teams against each other? Do you display favouritism?

Office politics are inevitable. Allowing them to breed and multiply into a toxic environment isn't.

3
Coping with the chaos.

Creative people are rarely fazed by chaos. This is a talent that will come in very useful to you as a creative director. Because you are going to experience a lot of it.

As you know, creativity is born of chaos. Great creative brains make connections in ways that no one else can. They connect the unconnectable. The more chaotic and messier their minds, the more likely these odd connections are to be made. Chaos is a wonderful, positive force for good, and it must be celebrated and protected. But it belongs in the creative process, not in the day of a creative director. Your job is to enable the chaos of creativity to flourish, while keeping the chaos of your role to a minimum.

Creative direction is without doubt a messy old business. Every year I promised myself that this would be the year I got it all under control. But I never got it all under control. Perhaps for a few fleeting moments, the odd week here and there, but never consistently. I always thought it was just me, and that I must be doing something wrong. Why couldn't I get ahead of everything and stay there? As soon as I had that pitch under control, I had a great team get headhunted, a shoot go sideways, a client panicking because her boss hated what she'd approved, and so on and so on. Chaos. Eventually, I realised that it's the same for everyone, it's just rarely admitted to. As a creative director, you don't want to look as though you aren't in control of everything. You believe it makes you look weak or incompetent. But that view must change. You can't control everything – no one can. It's not a failing on your part, it's because creativity and the creative process don't fit into tidy stacker-boxes or spreadsheets. They're amorphous and forever bursting at the seams and spilling out everywhere, meaning that there are just too many unforeseen and uncontrollable variables for harmony ever to exist in all of them at the same time. You must simply accept chaos as your constant companion, roll with it, and look after yourself.

The relentless pressure to create fresh, innovative work and to exert control over the process of achieving it leads to burnout and exhaustion if you don't take steps to prevent them. I lost count of how many weekends and holidays I spent recovering or feeling unwell, instead of relaxing and enjoying time with friends and family. Sound familiar? You can try to convince yourself that it's the price you pay for the job, but it shouldn't be. And it doesn't have to be. You will have to learn to let go and allow yourself to exert more control over fewer things. This may seem counter-intuitive, but it's the key to coping with the chaos.

There are a number of things you can do to make sure that creative chaos continues to do beautiful things, and you don't go under while it does them. These are simple, practical things that will enable you to keep the whole magnificent madness moving forward. They will help you to keep your energy levels up, lower your anxiety, extend your career and help you to foster more brilliant work. Feeling fresh and in control of the controllable aspects of the role will make you a far better creative director and, frankly, a much nicer person to be around. Don't say you haven't been warned.

You need enough CHAOS TO THRIVE, but enough ORDER TO SURVIVE.

Nadja Lossgott
Joint CCO, AMV BBDO London

Understand the stuff you need to just let CRASH AND BURN. There are some things you have to let go so that you have the mental energy to focus on the good stuff.

**Rodrigo Sobral
Global CCO, Oliver**

Does it really matter?

If not, don't do it. You're going to need to be able to distinguish between what matters to you and what matters to everyone else. You won't delight everyone in the process, but you will hang on to your sanity. Everything that comes your way will seem urgent or important or critical. In reality, some of it won't be any of those things, but people want to be heard, often believing that what they are doing is the most important thing ever. They may also have a very different idea of what constitutes urgent, important or critical than you do, and they will all make impassioned cases for why they need your undivided attention. Almost all the cases will seem like reasonable requests. Unfortunately, you simply won't have the time or headspace to treat everything equally.

You need a clear criterion for what you will do now, what you will do later, and what you want someone else to do for you. That criterion is up to you. But once you have it, stick to it, so that everyone is clear what it is and works with it. You'll be surprised how quickly people adapt if it's reasonable and you give them a viable option. They just want to be able to complete their task. My criterion was to prioritise issues that were in some way critical to creative quality or culture. That didn't mean that I waited until a situation was facing impending doom. It meant that I would act pre-emptively to ensure that things never got that far. But I kept my focus on the things that had the potential to turn into even bigger problems. I would also make sure that key people could get access to me when they needed it, so that important projects didn't bottleneck.

If you face into everything and try to please everyone, you'll just end up swamped and do a bad job of most of it. It's far better to be brilliant, considered and effective on 60% of things and delegate the other 40%, than to be a bit overwhelmed on 100%.

A right hand.

So, you've set your criterion for what is important to you. To make it work, you'll need someone to divert things to. It must be someone you trust to get the job done in the right way, or they will end up causing you more wasted time and trouble, not less. This is not a role for a maverick. It's for the most dependable person you have, the talented, safe pair of hands. They are someone who doesn't want to do your job, but whom everyone likes and respects. They are very rarely out-and-out leaders, but they're team players and they care deeply about the work and the success of the agency. They won't bristle at the stream of requests, but will work their way through them calmly and patiently. Finding someone you can trust to be your right hand will transform your ability to do your job. Not only can you divert some of the chaos their way, safe in the knowledge that it will be dealt with, but also you will have someone who is able to deputise for you when you're away, and someone to talk to when you need a little counsel. They are worth their weight in gold, so be good to them.

If you choose wisely, your right hand can perform another invaluable job for you. They will be able to tell you what other people aren't telling you. One of the dangers of the role in a medium-to-large agency is that you can become disconnected from the shop floor. Your time is spent in meetings, with clients, in pitches and presentations, on shoots, and so on, and time spent just shooting the breeze with the creative department is increasingly limited. And, in truth, they are probably quite guarded with you even when you do spend time with them, since you're their boss, not their mate. But your right hand is more likely to pop out for lunch with them or chat about how their day is going, and this is when you find out what everyone is really thinking: good, bad or indifferent. It can become a useful line of communication for everyone.

They are the LIFESAVER of all lifesavers.

Lynsey Atkin
Former CCO, McCann London

**Delegation is hard.
I think that's probably
one of the hardest things
as you switch paths.
Because you always feel like,
'I'LL JUST QUICKLY DO IT.'
And it's a disaster because
it makes everyone feel
they're not good enough
in your eyes. Honestly,
I don't want to work for
someone who doesn't
think I'm good enough.**

Nicholas Hulley
Joint CCO, AMV BBDO London

Delegate.

Finding your right hand is your first major step towards embracing delegation. But it's possible that you don't have that person to turn to, or that the demands are such that you'll need more help than they alone can offer.

It can take a little while to get the hang of putting your trust in others, especially for a control freak like you. But when you do, it's liberating, not only for you, but for everyone around you. Delegation is not a sign of weakness, it's a strength, and it shows confidence in your position. The best leaders are the best delegators. You will need to accept it as a necessary part of your job if you want to succeed.

If you need to build up your confidence in someone, start with delegating small things. This might be asking them to oversee the placement teams, give talks at colleges, go to the student shows, dedicate time to making sure that great young talent knows about and is interested in your agency or business. Or perhaps ask them to be on the agency party committee. These are all things that need time to do them justice – time that you don't have. Some of the happiest moments in my career came when I was trusted by the CCO to run a pitch or to help redesign the interior of the agency. It's a great way to build a trusted layer under you, and to give others space to grow.

If you choose not to delegate, you will in time create bottlenecks. Worse than that, important things will get kicked into the long grass and forgotten. Unfortunately, this is not uncommon in agencies. Whether through insecurity or through the mistaken belief that the creative director must control everything, you regularly find creative directors who create unnecessary problems for themselves. This can even stop an agency from functioning correctly. And yes, I and every creative director I know has made this mistake. It's almost a rite of passage.

Learning to let go.

You can't control what you can't control, however much you might want to. And there is a lot in this role that you can't control. That's tough for a control freak to accept. Even as you read this, you're shuddering at the thought of it. It's not going to be easy, because the desire to control our environment and circumstances is ingrained in all human beings; the more we can control our world, the safer we feel. And, as a sample of human beings, creative directors are at the more controlling end of things. So you will need to fight your evolutionary instincts or face feeling constantly out of control – which, psychologically, is not a sustainable place to be.

The 'self-help book' logic is that the more we strive for control of things we don't have power over, the more anxious we become. We respond by trying to control the situation even more, to counter our growing anxiety. If you let go of things you can't control, you will have a greater sense of peace and free up time and energy to focus on the things you can.

It all sounds great in principle, but I'm not sure I ever fully got to grips with this one. I always found it hard to work out exactly what it was that I couldn't control until I was in the middle of it, but I got better at it as time went on and I experienced more situations that proved to be outside my control. Through conversations with other creative directors, I've come to realise that this is the same for us all. It seems to be something of an exercise in trial and error. You just have to be disciplined with yourself and not repeat the mistake the next time a similar situation comes up. And stop beating yourself up about not being able to control everything. No one can – it's not a failing on your part. The one thing I did find helpful from my research into the self-help world of letting go was that you can control yourself, your own actions and reactions. That's a good place to start.

Thinking time.

You need to take self-care seriously. Burnout is real, and it doesn't discriminate. It's essential to build time into your diary to think your own thoughts. You'll feel as though this isn't possible, and the impending demands on your day will tell you it isn't possible, but you must make it possible. Aim for two or three hours a day.

I regularly had no free time from 9am until 6pm, five days a week. Up to fifteen meetings a day were crammed in, with few breaks. I was so exhausted by the end of the day that I wasn't able to give any thought to anything I had seen that day or needed to prep for the following day. Everything I did was reactive.

I was my own worst enemy for allowing this to happen. You have to block time in your diary and make everyone work around it. Talk it through with your leadership partners or account partners, and make sure they understand that they will have a much better version of you for a shorter period.

Thinking time enables you to respond in a more considered way to an issue, as well as increasing your focus and cognition. It lowers your blood pressure and heart rate, and reduces muscle tension, so that you're calmer, with a more positive frame of mind, instead of living on adrenaline. That benefits everyone around you. It also improves your sleep, which promotes mental and physical health and reduces days off for illness. It develops new brain cells in the hippocampus (the brain region associated with learning and memory), and it gives you an opportunity to refocus and be better prepared to handle your workload. So, far from being an indulgence, it's a necessity. It also allows you the chance to write creative ideas if you want to, and who doesn't want to? As all creatives know, quiet, undisturbed thinking time is when we are at our most creative. So go on, book it in.

Ask for help.

It's OK to admit that you don't know everything. It's not OK to pretend you do and then have something go wrong because of it. Making such an admission doesn't come easily to everyone – particularly creative directors in a corporate environment, where everyone is a little less open about their weaknesses than in a small, friendly indie – but it's surprisingly disarming and powerful if you have the courage to do it.

The reality is that no one can possibly know everything about every aspect of the advertising and communications industries, every channel, process, production technique, social platform protocol, and so on. Not only because it's so complex and varied, but also because it changes so fast. Learning new things is a constant state of being for a creative director, and as much as your creative curiosity drives you to want to know everything about everything, you don't have the time to acquire all that knowledge and become an expert.

You will need to be selective about what you commit your limited time to learning. For everything else, make a point of asking anyone who knows more about it than you do for their thoughts and advice. Not only will you learn something, but also it makes them feel valued, and you will save yourself a great deal of time and anxiety.

I recommend that you give serious consideration to where the weaknesses in your game are, and make sure that you have great people to turn to, and return to, when you need them. My Achilles heel is design. I'm a writer, and while I have strong opinions on art direction, design and photography, I would always have someone I trusted and who was better than me in these areas to turn to, someone who could inform my opinions. You're never too senior to learn from talented people.

One of the biggest things I learned early on is that IT'S OK NOT TO KNOW, as long as you're honest and say: 'I'm really not sure what we should do here.'

Richard Brim
Former CCO, Adam & Eve DDB London

Training.

You will never regret committing to continuous learning. What you learn will change as your needs change, but the need to stay informed and relevant is constant, especially for creative leaders. You probably feel you couldn't possibly fit more into your day than you do already, and that you've reached your capacity for assimilating new information. You may well be right. But consider allocating time to learning new skills that might help you to feel more relaxed in your role. A sense of chaos is often the result of a lack of understanding in a certain area, making it feel amorphous or impenetrable. The more you understand it, the less daunting and chaotic it seems and the more considered and productive you will be in dealing with it.

Of course this depends on what you're already good at and what you need help with, but try to focus on skills you need regularly for your role and haven't had any exposure to as a creative. Time management? Budget management? Conflict resolution? Negotiation? Presentation skills? It could also be fun stuff, such as photography or screenwriting, if you think this will make you a better creative director.

You don't need to become an expert; even a primer is better than nothing. You don't need to do everything all at once, either. Write a list and work your way through it when you can.

Perhaps start by asking your management team what they think you need to improve. It's common to be blind to your weaknesses, particularly if they are in unfamiliar areas, so you might not be aware of them. Not only will asking your leadership partners show a willingness to evolve, but also it shows a commitment to them. I would have huge respect for a management partner who came to me and asked what I thought they needed to work on.

There's a real deficit of people **LEARNING ON THE JOB** in the way they used to. Everyone's just so time-poor.

Scott Dungate
CCO, Uncommon London

It's ok to go home at
6 o'clock. It's actually
a really good idea.
I DON'T WORK LATE.
Normally I finish around
5.30. And I feel quite
comfortable doing it.

Alex Grieve
Global & London CCO, BBH

Looking after number one.

Looking after yourself is one of the best ways to stop the chaos from getting to you. It will also extend your career by keeping burnouts at bay. Don't think of it as being selfish; it really isn't. It will enable you to be your best self, and that's what everyone at work and at home wants and needs you to be.

It's easy to slip into being a martyr to the demands of the role. Your relentless pursuit of better and fresher can drive you to believe that you have to exhaust yourself of every ounce of your energy before you can stop. We've all done it. But if you keep doing it, the job will swallow you whole.

You also need something to lose yourself in outside work, something that enables you to forget all about creative directing and switch off those parts of your brain that are getting overused. It could be painting, football, whatever. For me, it was hanging out with horses. It doesn't matter what it is, as long as it forces you to be in the here and now and not dwell on work. If you don't have a passion for something outside work, develop one, quickly. The other benefit to having interests is that you will gain fresh perspectives to bring to your work.

Trips and holidays are essential too, so forward-plan them. There are two main benefits of planning your leave early. One is that you can break your year down into more manageable chunks. Knowing that you are working towards time away really helps with the psychology of coping. The second is that by planning ahead you can make sure you have the right cover in place so that you don't spend all your time away being interrupted by work calls, or leave everyone suffering the consequences of you not planning ahead. There will never be a right time to take a holiday. It will always affect something that matters at work. But that's where delegation comes in. Never give up your holiday. Ever.

Mentor.

Throughout my career I was fortunate enough to have a couple of my ex-CCOs to turn to for advice. I'd pick their brains about something that was troubling me or ask their advice about a job I'd been approached about, or how to deal with a situation I'd not come across before. I often knew the answer already, but having them either challenge or validate my thinking was always invaluable. 'Never roll your tanks on their lawn' was my favourite piece of advice from one of them when I asked how, as a fledgling creative director, to deal with senior creatives.

Any senior person worth their salt will be more than happy to mentor you. It's flattering to be asked, and it takes up very little time. It's generally best to have someone you know well from outside your agency, who will offer a fresh and untainted view. I wish now that I had been more systematic with my mentors. I was quite ad hoc about it and consequently didn't benefit from their wisdom as much as I might have done. Try to make it a regular meeting, even if you don't have a burning question. For the price of a few breakfasts or coffees you will get access to some great, considered and personalised counselling.

It's also worth considering a creative coach or an exec coach. Many larger agencies are happy to pay for this kind of support, and if yours isn't, it's worth considering paying for it yourself. The ability to discuss something with a knowledgeable outsider, or to confide in someone who isn't caught up in the pressures and politics of your day, is truly invaluable. They will help you to return to your values to assess decisions you've made or approaches you've taken, enabling you to review them yourself and adjust if necessary. Even the best creative director gets it wrong sometimes. Don't beat yourself up about it, but it's important to learn from it. You'll only do that with the right help.

Write a to-do list.

This is without doubt the most mundane piece of advice in the entire book. Nevertheless, I decided to include it because it genuinely makes a difference. Writing a to-do list may be the last thing you want to do before you leave your desk at night or first thing in the morning. But look at it as an essential part of your day, a task that will save you a lot of time in the long run. You won't be able to keep everything in your head. I've tried – it gets mixed up or forgotten and creates avoidable inefficiency and anxiety. Seeing it written down in a list is extremely calming. And there are few more satisfying things in life than ticking jobs off the list when you complete them.

Everyone will have their own way of organising their list, but I broke mine down into 'Work' and 'Life'. I started out by keeping my list on my laptop, but for some reason I ended up rarely referring to it. This, it turns out, is common, despite all the integrated to-do-list tools and apps that are available. So I bought an A5 Moleskine notebook and a pencil with a rubber on top, and never looked back. (The reason for the pencil is that it makes it far less messy to make the million changes that you're going to make.) I kept everything in that notebook: my to-do list, ideas for clients, notes from meetings, references, random ideas. Everything that would otherwise have been cluttering up my head.
It meant that in quiet moments I could reflect on what I'd done, what I needed to do, and the interesting things I'd heard that day. I always wrote a list for the week on a Sunday afternoon or evening as a way of planning ahead, and added and subtracted as the week went on.
I got through about three books a year and kept them for at least a year after they were full, just in case. I know other people who still have every single one they've ever filled up.

4
What does everyone expect from me?

The greatest amplifier of disappointment is expectation. So, before you can manage – or, ideally, exceed – everyone's expectations of you as a creative leader, you need to understand what those expectations are. Let's start with the basics. Everyone expects you to be a beacon of creative energy. How you live up to that expectation has many facets that are discussed throughout this book.

The focus for this chapter, however, is on the specific expectations that people in different roles and departments across the agency have of you. As a general rule, these expectations are driven by selfish motivations. Everyone needs and wants something different from you if they are to succeed in their role, and they don't want you messing it up for them. They can sometimes be at odds with other people's expectations, so you won't be able to please everyone, but at least if you know what they are you can deal with them.

When I started out in the role of creative director, before I ran an agency, I lacked the self-awareness to realise that everyone had expectations of me. At that point I only really saw it from my own point of view, which was that they were there mostly to enable me to shine in my role. Over the years I learned that the more I understood what others expected from me, the more I could help them to succeed, and consequently the more I would succeed.

Like it or not, people have hopes and beliefs about what they want you to do or not do for them. These are rarely based on an agreed measure, but rather on what they have determined they need from you, or on their previous experience, often without knowing or considering your ability, capacity or personality. Unsurprisingly, for that reason we often fail to meet other people's expectations of us and, through no fault of our own, lose their trust in our abilities.

For clarity, expectations are a one-sided visualisation of what the future might be, based on assumptions. There is a critical difference between expectations and having shared criteria for behaviour or performance.

Never assume. When in doubt, ask what people want or need in each situation. Over-communicate. Don't leave anything to chance. This works both ways, so also make it clear what you need and expect from them. 'Assumption is the mother of all fuck-ups,' as Travis Dane famously said in the otherwise forgettable movie *Under Siege 2*. Let others know exactly what your strengths and weaknesses are, what you're capable of, where you're flexible and where you aren't. Try to turn expectations on both sides into agreed and understood behaviours or actions. The more clarity there is, the better.

It's often said that the only thing worse than knowing someone's expectations of you is not knowing them. Knowing at least means you have an opportunity to manage the expectations towards what you can actually deliver.

I've written this chapter from the perspective of a CCO, but it translates to every level of creative leader. It will give you an understanding of what people expect from you. To even it up, each section includes what you should reasonably expect from others, too. Use it as a conversation starter with the people in each role, to get them to talk about their expectations of you and your expectations of them. You can then have a realistic conversation about what you can deliver for each other, giving you both the opportunity to under-promise and over-deliver.

The creative director has all the hopes and expectations of the agency heaped on their shoulders. They are the ones who everyone expects will have an answer even when no one else does. They're SUPERMAN, YOUR MUM AND LEONARDO DA VINCI ALL ROLLED INTO ONE. The unrealistic expectation is what creates the stress.

Kevin Chesters
CSO, KC Consulting

The CEO.

The CEO (Chief Executive Officer) will expect more of you than of anyone else in the building. They will expect you to be the brightest creative talent in the department, but also the most generous; the most compelling speaker, and at the same time the most active listener. They will expect you to be a leader for every department, not just the creative department; to be a beacon for everyone, including the clients and the industry press. They will expect you to be aware of the key drivers of business success and to be adaptable to them, yet creatively uncompromising. They will expect you to understand your responsibility to build an inclusive and creative culture. And they will expect you to do all that in a measured yet passionate way, ideally with a smile on your face.

Faced with so much expectation, what you should expect in return is that they want you to win and will work tirelessly to make sure you do. They will work with you to create a shared value system and criteria for success. They will trust you, back you and dust you off when you fall.

You should both expect that you will always have each other's back. If you don't, it's going to be bumpy. Because CCOs are hired by the CEO, the CEO is technically your boss as well as your partner. But you should expect them only ever to feel like your partner; if they feel like your boss, something is wrong. They won't necessarily expect to be involved in creative leadership hires other than yours, but to set your creative directors up for success, it makes sense to involve the CEO in the process.

CEOs expect their creative partner and all the creative leaders to take an active role in driving the whole agency forward, not just their own careers.

What do I expect? As much interest in the strategy and the client's business as in the work. I expect that they will be **PASSIONATE ABOUT THE PROBLEMS** we're trying to solve, not just the work we're trying to make.

Katie Mackay-Sinclair
Partner, Mother London

If you've got the
PERFECT COMBINATION,
that relationship between
strategy leader and
creative leader is magic.
Because both of you
want each other to win.

Rob Campbell
CSO, Colenso NZ

The CSO.

If they are smart, the CSO will know that the most important relationship in their working life is with you. And vice versa. I must be honest here and say that this is my single favourite agency relationship. A great CSO is worth their weight in gold lions to you. They will help you in so many ways to elevate the creative output, not by having a creative opinion on it, but by finding the insights and developing the jumping-off points that will get you to fresh places. Then, as you develop work, they will help you by keeping you honest to the strategy, or by realising that the work has surpassed the original strategy and, without ego, reworking the brief to support the work. They make great presenting partners when it comes to selling work, too. Head and heart: anchoring the logic while you sell the dream. They're also brilliant at constructing arguments to protect the work through all the client and research hoops, then writing the awards submissions and narrative structures for case studies.

Your CSO will expect a number of things in return for all this. They will expect you to bring as much passion for the development of the strategy as you do for the creative work. They will expect you to commit publicly to the brief and make great work from it, not treat it as a barrier to overcome and undermine their thinking. They also want to see that getting to a great answer matters to you, and that you will give everything in pursuit of it. Because if you don't, why should they? The last thing you want is to demoralise them. They know you are the only person who can shine a light on their work. Strategy is rarely famous if the work isn't good enough to draw attention to it. CSOs expect you to be open to building a relationship of equals with them. They know that their role is in service of the creative output, but don't expect them to be servile. The good ones never are.

The CPO.

In most cases the CPO (Chief Production Officer, or Head of Production; titles vary) reports to the CCO, so you should have a degree more control of this relationship. I once asked my CPO how she would define her role, and she replied, 'Get shit done, beautifully.' You may be the architect of the work, but the CPO is the contractor who makes sure your vision is realised to the highest standards the budget allows.

You will need to establish that you have a shared idea of how 'excellent' looks or you're destined for a difficult relationship. Don't rush into that judgement; all kinds of things could have impacted how they went about their job previously, so ideally wait to see it for yourself in practice. They know that their role depends on you seeing eye to eye. And if you do, the CPO is one of your greatest allies and assets. When they feel trusted, they bring an immense amount of creativity and problem-solving to the party. Ask their views on work constantly and be open to their thoughts. Talk through work before it goes to clients, and ask their advice on production approaches. The more you involve them, the better the outcome will be.

The CPO is under pressure to deliver on time, on budget and on point, so they will be looking to you to enable them to succeed. They will expect you to be decisive, because indecision costs money, slows production and affects momentum, all outcomes that mean they will be judged as doing a poor job. They will also expect you to be able to articulate clearly what you want so that they can pursue the right solutions. Together you will need to strike a pragmatic balance between creative vision and the reality of budget and time, and work openly to make the most of both. They expect you to be creatively demanding, but at the same time adaptable and resilient to the ebbs and flows of production. Whatever stage of your creative leadership career you are at, you will need the CPO on your side.

You need a creative director to be **DECISIVE** about things. But then be **ADAPTABLE** and **RESILIENT** as you go through the ever-changing production process to get to the endgame.

Charlie Gatsky Sinclair
President Brands & Entertainment, Uncommon

There are some creative directors who get their followership because they have the work behind them. So, there is that earned trust. I'M GOING TO LISTEN TO YOU because I can see that you have done it before. And there are some who have a followership because they're compelling and they are able to bring out the best in other people.

Nicholas Hulley
Joint CCO, AMV BBDO London

The creative department.

The creative department will understandably have exceedingly high expectations of you. They will also be the least forgiving, simply because you hold their careers in your hands. No one has a greater impact on their future than you.

They expect you to stand up for creativity at every turn, to fight tooth and nail for the best work and to hold everyone in the agency to account if it isn't achieved. They expect you to know what to do in any situation, and always to know what constitutes great work and how to achieve it. They expect you to understand them, support them, celebrate them, get the best out of them and reward them.

If you don't do all those things simultaneously, daily, they will moan about you behind your back. In fact, they will probably do that anyway.

They aren't generally aware of the pressures of operating margins, budgets, client organisational politics and so on that can affect creative ambition (or if they are, they're not interested in them). They just expect you to sort out that stuff and create an environment in which they can selfishly do brilliant work that will make their name, win them awards, earn them more money, build their careers and possibly one day allow them to get your job. In an industry where famous, award-winning work is the currency, I don't consider these expectations unreasonable. In truth, you should want the creative department to think that way, because the greater their ambition to do great work, the better it is for everyone, including you.

The only way you will ever live up to their expectations is if you help them to make good work. All your other imagined failings will then be overlooked. All creatives want to do good work, and they expect you to help make it happen.

The global CCO.

Fortunately, the role of the global CCO has changed a great deal over the last few years. The new generation are profoundly different from the old ones. They tend to be creative and cultural nurturers, not aloof figures of fear or awards despots, and they are keen to build strong, collegiate relationships with their local creative leaders. If you are in an organisation that has a CCO like this, they can be a fantastic resource. Expect them to help you navigate complicated client organisations, find ways to get great work made, mentor and advise you, and channel opportunities into your office.

The role of the global CCO is to set the creative and cultural agenda for the network, and they will expect you to deliver on it locally. They are tasked with keeping creative and cultural standards high globally, but rarely control whether a local creative leader is hired or fired, and in truth are not empowered to take direct action against any of your decisions. So they can succeed only through influence and creating a willing followership. Consequently, they will expect you to actively lean in, to be communicative, collaborative and willing to be involved in group projects if you are asked. They won't appreciate you being reluctant to share updates on client relationships and work. The more open and positive you are with them, the more they can help you, so always overshare rather than undershare.

It's also a good idea to seek their counsel, since there aren't many people who are willing to give you honest, informed feedback on what and how you are doing. This is particularly valuable when it comes from people who have done the role successfully and have a vested interest in helping you to win. You don't technically answer to them, but they can make your life easier or harder depending on how much of an effort you make with them. They are another smart, talented person who is in a position to help you succeed. Don't pass up the opportunity.

The planning department.

I've always been a big fan of planning departments and planners. I have enormous respect for the brilliantly instinctive and culturally aware ones who use data only to support their intuition. The ones who are willing to get it wrong in pursuit of something different and exciting, who are interested in planning not as an exercise in intellectual one-upmanship but as a springboard to the best work.

Great creative planners expect you to engage early in the process. They enjoy working with you to develop the brief; they expect you to debate their thinking, test their logic and sharpen their language. There are few things more demotivating to them than just nodding and telling them to get it briefed in, or saying it's rubbish, just do it again. To paraphrase the philosopher Bertrand Russell, ordinary planners are very sure of themselves, but great planners are full of doubt. The good ones want your input and need your validation, because they know the brief won't get far without it.

Make sure they know that you'll only ever accept a brief if you believe it will lead somewhere interesting. But once you do, treat it like a contract. Stick to it. And if creative development shows that it needs to change, talk it through with the planning department. They will expect – or at least hope – that you are generous with your time, explain your thinking, and help them to understand how you see the world and what you want to achieve from the brief. They know that they will learn as much from you as they will from their CSO or Head of Planning.

It's important that you build trust with the entire planning department, and that they feel valued by you. Collaborate closely with them. Inspire and challenge them. Praise them publicly. Building a wall between creativity and planning will only ever end badly for you and the work.

The account management department.

One of the biggest differences between great creative agencies and not great creative agencies is the quality of account management. Despite that, the tension that frequently exists between creative leaders and account management is notorious. Account management has rather lost its confidence as a discipline in recent years, eroded by project management, creative directors becoming central to client relationships, financial transparency and the growing influence of planning. They have less reach than they once did, but they are nevertheless still vital in creating the conditions for creative risk-taking.

Great account people are motivated by the work, just like you. They know that enabling it wherever possible builds brand and agency fame in equal measure, attracting new clients, talent and revenue in the process. How you view account management and what you expect of each other comes down to the type of agency you are in. In agencies that prioritise client service, account management will expect you to be creatively innovative but willing to compromise without too much fuss. In agencies that prioritise creativity, on the other hand, account management will expect you to be creatively innovative and will do everything they can to avoid you having to compromise the work.

They expect different things of you because they are under different pressures, yet you expect the same support from them. Therein lies the tension. The reality is that advertising is an oversupplied market, and if you don't do what a client wants, someone else will. No account person wants to lose business. So, unless you are at an agency famed for its creativity and the clients are there for that reason and your strategy is to make famous work, you should either consider your position or review the agency vision and agenda with your leadership team. It's pointless beating up on account management.

I really hate hearing phrases like 'the suits' and all that old-school language. It's derogatory to what they do. **THEY DO AN AMAZING JOB.** If you've ever done a project where you haven't got an account person, you definitely feel it very, very fast.

Scott Dungate
CCO, Uncommon London

The client.

The first and most important expectation any client has is that you will listen to them and make every effort to understand exactly what they need. They have come to you because you have the skills they don't, and it's these creative skills that will answer that need, so it matters that you grasp the ask and demonstrate your understanding through the work. But this is an expectation that is not considered in these terms as often as it could be. You will take clients much further with you on the creative journey if they feel it's in pursuit of answering their needs rather than yours. The most successful creative agencies have always recognised this.

Even the very best clients can become anxious about the work, simply because they aren't in complete control of it yet their careers and reputation are bound to it. They will expect you to be passionate about their brand, to be excited by its possibilities and ambitious for its potential – and not just because they are paying you to be. They will expect that it matters to you almost as much as it matters to them, because if it doesn't you won't insist on the best people in your team working on it, or that the agency pulls out all the stops to do an incredible job. No client expects their relationship with their creative director to be transactional.

In return, you should expect to be able to have a fair and considered dialogue about the work. You can't expect trust, but you can expect to earn it, and that the world won't return to zero with every new project. Once you've earned that trust, you should expect to build a lasting relationship that leads to consistently good work and an increasing opportunity to push the creative ambition.
It's a fair exchange of expectations.

Agency partners.

No agency exists in isolation from the rest of the industry. Whether it's working with a production company, a media company, headhunters or any number of other businesses, you need to build trusted relationships. There are two main reasons for that. First, when you're under pressure to deliver, it makes life a lot easier if you have people around you whom you know you can rely on, and who will go out of their way to make sure you succeed. Second, it's a small industry and everyone talks. The more people speak positively about you and how you go about your business, the better, often in the most tangential ways. Having industry influencers who want you to win is a powerful asset.

To build up that network, those businesses will have clear expectations of you, too. A maxim you must live up to is 'Do as you would be done by.' They will expect you to treat them fairly, pay them promptly and show their team the same professional respect that they show you. The moment you don't, they'll be gone. Or, worse, they'll just see you as a paying job and do only what is needed. They will also tell everyone that you're a bit of a bellend. No bridge is ever burned in our industry without lots of people hearing about it.

In the cut and thrust of your busy day, it can be easy to slip into being demanding and not bothering to thank people, especially when they do a great job for you. Agency partners know you're busy and that you're being pulled in many different directions, but their expectations will need to be met or exceeded.

Take the time and trouble to build this network and to help its members as much as they help you. It's a simple and reasonable expectation that you can have of each other.

Yourself.

Creative people constantly compare themselves to other creatives and end up convinced that they are falling short in one way or another. We're world-class when it comes to beating ourselves up for not living up to our often unrealistic expectations of ourselves. This is mostly because we all suffer with varying degrees of imposter syndrome (yes, even that incredible creative director who you think has it all), which is triggered by there being no right or wrong in creativity, only your informed but subjective judgement of what you believe will work in a given set of circumstances. We would do well to remember that if there were actually an equation that guaranteed famous, award-winning creative work every time, technology would have replaced us by now. There isn't. There's just us, our taste and judgement, and hard work.

As you will by now be aware, everyone has expectations of you, some reasonable, some not. I recommend that you don't add to the burden by having expectations of yourself. You're ambitious or you wouldn't be where you are, but it won't help you achieve those ambitions by placing unrealistic demands on yourself. They will just eat away at you. Replace them with goals or objectives.

There's a big difference between goals and expectations. Goals are quantifiable, based on reality and fact; expectations are aspirations based on hope and opinion. Goals are great things to set yourself, while expectations will mostly end up making you feel as though you've failed. Don't do it to yourself. Set yourself clear and achievable goals, like hiring a great team or improving your pitch success rate. Allow yourself the chance to feel you're making progress. Don't set the expectation that you'll be the most awarded creative in the history of adland.

I think all creative directors have that sense that they're MAKING IT UP as they go along.

Felix Richter
CCO, Mother London

5
Building and running a creative department.

Introverted, extroverted, erratic, opinionated, monosyllabic, eccentric, arrogant, underconfident, hyperactive, lazy. Anything but straightforward. Creative departments are full of wonderfully complicated people, and it's your job now to get the best out of them all. Ideally, all at the same time. You could, of course, just hire and promote people who are compliant and easy to manage, but I suspect your creative output won't set the world on fire if you do.

Managing great creative talent is a privilege, but also unbelievably and unavoidably frustrating. Most creative people are independent and rebellious by nature, making them distrustful of management and being managed. So you must give careful consideration to how you're going to manage them. Over the course of my first few years in creative leadership, I learned that the more I tried to manage them, unsurprisingly, the more they reacted against being managed. Eventually, I realised that to succeed I would need not only to create the right environment for brilliant work to flourish, but also to give creatives the freedom to enjoy it.

I should have known that from the start, really, since that was how I needed to be treated to function at my best. It's easy for me to look back at that behaviour and be self-critical, but when you first find yourself in charge of a department or a few teams, it's not uncommon to feel you must impose yourself. It can take a little while to get used to the weight of responsibility for creative work that you aren't in complete control of. As I discovered, the more you try to act like the boss, the less the creative department will respect you and want to deliver for you. The reality is that you are now in service to them. They will respect you for nurturing, supporting and championing them, not for giving them orders.

The best chance you have of successfully leading a department is to accept creative people for who and what they are. Work with their idiosyncrasies, not against them. Embrace their unpredictability, rather than trying to regiment them. Don't force them to follow processes or structures that constrain them. Let them work remotely and outside normal hours. Don't ask where they are, what they are doing or how they do it. As long as they deliver and their work is good enough, manage them as lightly as possible. The good ones will rise to it, and those who don't might need to be moved on.

You have, of course, been in creative departments your entire career. Some will have had great cultures but no ambition, while others with nasty cultures did incredible work. If you're lucky, one or two had great cultures and did great work. Now that you're in charge, you will be the biggest single influence on which yours is.

You'll have to find your own way of allowing people creative freedom while maintaining control of the outcome, and of tolerating risk without letting it get out of hand. You're now not only in service to the creative department, but also to the overall well-being of the agency, and that can, at times, be a conflicted position.

You will need to give a great deal of thought to the environment you want to create, and how to create it. You will undoubtedly have your own ideas and experiences to bring to it. The points in this chapter are the result of many years of trial and error managing teams as well as building, rebuilding and maintaining productive and successful creative departments. They will give you the confidence to inspire confidence in the department. They will help you to show that you have their best interests at heart, and not just your own. They will guide you in setting parameters without denying freedom. Most importantly of all, they will enable you to build a department that is energised and focused on producing great work.

It's not about proving to anyone how **BRILLIANT, POWERFUL AND SUCCESSFUL** you are. It's almost like the opposite.

**Alex Grieve
Global & London CCO, BBH**

Responsibility, not power.

Don't confuse having responsibility with having power. This is the single most important piece of advice in the book. (That's why I reference it several times.) It doesn't matter what else you do; if you get this wrong you will fail. It's easy to get swept up in the cachet of being made a CD/ECD/CCO. These are glamorous and aspirational roles, so it's hardly surprising or even unusual to start believing you're a little bit special. You may well be, but that doesn't give you any special privileges when it comes to how you treat the people who work for you.

Throwing your weight around in an environment where no one feels able to stand up to you for fear of reprisal is catastrophic for both your reputation and the functioning of the department. And it will very quickly be your undoing if you continue with it. Behaviour like that comes from a lack of confidence, and the department will spot it a mile off. No one gives their all for someone they don't like or feel valued by. You will be busy and under pressure most of the time, but if you ever treat your teams with anything other than humility and respect you will lose them and with them all hope of getting great work out. As I mentioned in the introduction to this chapter, you are now in service to the department. They are looking to you to be someone they can trust to act fairly, someone who is capable of inspiring them. You become a leader only when people are willing to follow you. Not when they are forced to. You are there to lift them up, not the other way round.

Good leadership is always open to challenge, rather than seeking to crush it. That proves you're willing to listen and have respect for others' views. In the words of former British prime minister Margaret Thatcher – who is rarely, if ever, quoted in a creative context – 'Being powerful is like being a lady. If you have to say you are, you aren't.'

The best creative leaders are able to tell **HARD TRUTHS KINDLY** and make people feel comfortable with uncertainty.

**Katie Mackay-Sinclair
Partner, Mother London**

Drop your ego and don't think that JUST BECAUSE YOU'RE IN CHARGE it's your responsibility to do absolutely everything even if you're not very good at it. One of the key things about being a creative director is actually getting out of the way and allowing people their own space and time to do things, but then having the knowledge so that, if things go wrong or they need support, you're there to help them out.

Alex Grieve
Global & London CCO, BBH

Direction, not dictation.

Telling creatives exactly what the answer to a brief is and using them to write it up for you is probably the most common accusation levelled at a creative director, and without doubt, it's the most common mistake creative directors make. The mitigation for it is that they feel responsible for delivering on every brief, and in the absence of an answer it's their job to provide one. But, if they're being completely honest, it can also be because everyone believes their own ideas are brilliant. In behavioural science this is called the IKEA Effect, and it's a terminal habit to get into.

     It's tough to get it right every time, though. Finding the balance between having a clear vision for your client's brand that you want executed a certain way, and telling teams what you want and exactly how you want it, must be viewed case by case. Your job is to know what is needed and to make sure it is delivered, but if you don't allow space for other views or interpretations you will not only put unsustainable pressure on yourself through always having to have the answer, but also demotivate everyone around you. They are the 'creative department', not the 'second-guessing the creative director department'. It pays to have strong opinions lightly held, since the one thing you can be certain of is that if you let them, teams will surprise you with something brilliant, something you'd never have thought of. That is their job, so make sure you're open to being challenged by it.

     It's only when they don't find the answer that you can dictate what needs to be done. Remember that this is a last resort. Use it sparingly; dictatorships are not positive environments in the long term and only result in departments full of browbeaten creatives who are waiting for you to tell them what to do, then dialling it in, while looking for other jobs. And when that happens, you're in trouble.

Hire in haste, repent at leisure.

Finding people you like, rate, believe will prosper in your department, and want to come to your agency is challenging, but it's an awful lot harder to get rid of them. So do your homework. First, establish if they are actually responsible for the work they are claiming. The collaborative nature of the industry means it's not uncommon for creatives to claim credit for work when they had little to do with it. Take references with a pinch of salt, too. Who ever put down as a reference someone who wouldn't sing their praises? The business is a small one, and there's a good chance that by now you know a lot of people in it. Find someone who has worked with the candidate, whether first or second hand. At the very least you'll get confirmation of their character.

You will not have a pot of money sitting around that you can dip into whenever you feel like it (see Chapter 9). You are going to have to fight for hires, pay rises and bonuses, and you will constantly be making a case for why you need more and better resources. So when you do find someone who is worth the effort, make sure you get the salary pre-approved, as well as bonuses and perks. Nothing puts off someone who is in demand more quickly than a flaky hiring process. If you can try before you buy to ensure a cultural and creative fit, so much the better.

Even when you aren't hiring, try to keep a slot in your diary for meeting teams. You never know when you might need one, and it's useful to have a shortlist in mind, but also this gives you a chance to tell good teams what you and your agency are doing, which is great for creative community PR. CDs and ECDs should also try to see lots of student teams, partly because they need the advice and support you can give them, and partly because every department benefits from having a student intern or placement programme.

Give me a team with the right attitude. Teams that have done really good work in not-so-good agencies. Because they've battled and they've scrapped and given everything to make that work happen. ALL THE PEOPLE I RESPECT HAVE AT SOME POINT BEEN IN A SHIT AGENCY. It teaches you to be relentless. You become a fighter.

Richard Brim
Former CCO, Adam & Eve DDB London

Avoiding the mini-me syndrome.

It's a common mistake in creative leadership to be drawn to hiring creative teams that are like you. It's also completely understandable; it's human nature to like people who like the same things as us, who laugh at the same jokes or share the same passions. It's reassuring and comfortable. But you must push back against that urge. Mini-me departments are dangerously myopic. Everyone thinking in the same way, with the same cultural references and interests, reduces your collective ability to do something different or surprising.

You often hear the expression 'hire your weakness'. That should be your starting point: to hire people who aren't like you at all. Matthew Syed wrote a brilliant book about this, *Rebel Ideas: The Power of Diverse Thinking* (2019). In it he shows how in a modern, multicultural world full of complex, layered problems, it's a distinct disadvantage to have similarly educated, similarly raised people solving the issues. They will all have the same blind spots, the same prejudices and the same sensibilities. To keep things fresh, develop a diverse range of personalities and voices.

Consider gender, ethnicity, age, neurodiversity and physical diversity. But also think about different life experiences and backgrounds. In the UK, the number of working-class creatives in the industry is now less than half of what it was fifty years ago, for a range of restrictive economic reasons. So go out of your way to find and encourage them; they are fast becoming an unheard voice in the creative industries, yet working-class people account for more than half of the population.

Challenge yourself on every hire. Can they do something that you can't? Do they bring a new perspective or set of references? Will they bring something to the department that you don't have already? And will they stir up some healthy competition?

I always find a mini-me, but I just need one or two of them and that is enough me. I need a mini-me because there are moments when you'll have a flash of an idea, and you need someone who gets your style of humour or prose and you can say 'What about this?' and they come back in three hours with a deck that has everything you talked about. But once you've got your mini-me, **FOR THE LOVE OF GOD, GET YOURSELF A FRENCH ART DIRECTOR** and a Brazilian activation specialist and a power writer – you know, someone who can write stuff that makes you weep – all the superpowers you wish you had. All of a sudden you will have this cabinet of wonders that gives your agency range, so there's nothing you can't tackle, no account you can't take on.

Chris Beresford-Hill
Global CCO, BBDO

It's very different at Mother from at Droga. And I've adapted to the Mother way because I was surprised at how well it works. At Droga, the process was creative team and creative director for a couple of rounds, then the ECD or David, then an 'internal' with everyone involved. At Mother, every meeting has everyone in it. It's the round sofa idea. So everybody is there from the start. When I heard about it, I was like, 'That must be so stressful for a junior creative team to be in front of ten people.' But it's surprising how it works. **PEOPLE HERE HAVE INCREDIBLE MEETING DISCIPLINE.** And it largely works very similarly to the other way, where it's the team presenting, the creative director mostly talking and talking first, then everybody else giving essentially the same comments that come later in the Droga process, in the internal reviews. It's interesting because we had two very different processes that became very similar. As long as the creative director speaks first, and it's not just problems first, it works.

Felix Richter
CCO, Mother London

Reviews.

Don't worry if you find reviews a little stressful. They are stressful. Everyone finds them stressful. Stress isn't always a bad thing, by the way; the right level of stress makes everyone operate at a higher level. And that's the type of stress you want in a review – the positive kind, where expectations are high but everyone wants everyone else to win. Whether that is how the review turns out is up to you. Building on people's thinking rather than tearing it down publicly is the surest way to get a good outcome.

    Everyone gets nervy in the build-up to a review. The teams are hoping they have delivered on the brief. The account team and planners are hoping the teams have delivered on the brief (although their idea of delivering might be quite different from the creatives'). And you're hoping to see something exciting that transcends the brief and gets everyone in the agency excited. Or, failing that, that you will be able to think quickly enough to spot a grain of something that can be developed into something that gets everyone in the agency excited.

    I'm not sure anyone but the creative director realises how much pressure the creative director is under in a creative review. You're expected to show an insightful understanding of all the creative, cultural, contextual and business factors that go into spotting the right work, take everyone with you, keep the teams feeling excited to develop it, and give everyone the confidence that you have it all under control.

    Spotting great work and helping the team to get it into the best shape possible is probably the single biggest high you will have as a creative director. It always was for me, because it lifted the whole agency, not just that particular team. Everyone wants to feel they work somewhere that is capable of doing great things. Reviews are the moment when those great things are revealed.

Appraisals.

There are two schools of thought on creative appraisals. Some creative directors feel the teams are constantly being appraised in reviews and don't like the formality of an appraisal, while others like the opportunity to have a structured conversation about career development. Whichever view you take, make sure you are regularly giving creatives feedback on how they are doing. Never allow these sessions to become awkward or combative. Consider structuring appraisals as an opportunity to communicate your vision and expectations and how the individual or team are doing against them.

Communication with your teams is critical. You are extremely important to them. They want you to think they are doing well, and if they aren't, they want you to help them fix it. When I was a CD, I had a CCO who didn't talk to me for the first six months I worked for him. He'd smile and nod in passing, but that was it. It really troubled me. I kept saying to my wife, 'I don't know what I've done, but I don't think he likes me much.' I had young kids and a mortgage, and was getting worried that I'd be fired. I couldn't for the life of me understand why he was ignoring me; I'd won a huge pitch, was doing really good work and winning awards, and felt I fitted in well. I called the headhunters and said it was draining my confidence, that I thought I should look to move. They suggested I ask him why the silence before doing anything drastic, because it was a great agency and it would be tough to match the role. So I asked him. His answer: 'What? It's going great. Couldn't be happier. Why would I need to speak to you about it?'

Everyone in the creative industries worries about job security. It's notoriously volatile. Reassuring people who are doing a good job will give them the confidence to take the creative risks you need them to take, and giving clear guidance to those who need it will make them more productive.

Whoever comes on your journey, YOU OWE IT TO THEM to give them a curated career mentorship.

**Charlie Gatsky Sinclair
President Brands & Entertainment, Uncommon**

Celebrate the work.

Advertising, communications and design are not service industries. We are manufacturing industries. We make a product. The quality of that product has the ability to change the fortunes of everyone associated with it, from the client to the junior producer. Everyone in the agency benefits from making that product as brilliant as it can be. It is the manifestation of all the blood, sweat and tears that were poured into winning the account, developing the relationships, the late nights and weekends of strategic and creative development, the stress of the presentations, the feedback, the rewrites, production, post-production, more feedback and screaming deadlines, so it deserves to be celebrated. Everyone who played a part in getting the work out into the world should be carried shoulder-high around the agency and cheered.

Celebrating everyone's hard work and achievements is essential to fostering an ambitious creative culture and making everyone want to keep making a brilliant product. In an incredibly competitive creative industry, it's also important to celebrate creativity more publicly as a way of signalling your intent as an agency. Don't forget: it matters hugely that your team feels proud to work somewhere their friends wished they worked, and where other people are jealous of the work you do, work that gets written and talked about.

Whether through entering awards, hosting talks or exhibitions, or doing agency-initiative projects, you need to make creative excellence the department's North Star, and reward and inspire the creative department to live up to it. Make creativity the most important topic in the building and sharing great examples of it an everyday event, and you will ignite ambition and competition. Then make it clear where you are setting the bar, and when it's reached, go all out.

Always have their backs.

Creative directors who throw creatives working for them under the bus to protect themselves from criticism are a disgrace to the role. Don't do it. Simple as that. It might be a short-term face-saving win for a creative director, but it's a big, long-term reputational loss. That sort of behaviour rips through a department in seconds. You'll never be able to earn back that trust or shake the tag of being snaky. This is also a small, very interconnected industry, and the more people who speak well of you as a creative director and of your department culture, the better. News of bad behaviour spreads much more quickly than news of good behaviour.

It helps no one if you're known to turn on your teams. The department needs to know that you have their back. It's not about closing ranks and protecting your own; it's about demonstrating that they matter to you, and that you trust and respect them enough to stand up for them. Don't underestimate how much it will matter to the teams. Being a creative in an agency is stressful. A lot is expected of you in a short time, again and again, and no one can get it right all the time. So, knowing that you are supportive of your teams genuinely reduces stress levels, it even lowers blood-pressure reactivity (the way blood pressure responds to stress). It creates a more productive and encouraging environment and ultimately better work.

If criticism of you is fair, hold your hands up. Take it and fix it publicly. But if criticism of your department or individual teams is justified, accept it publicly and deal with it privately. The buck stops with you. You are responsible for hiring them, training them, developing them, inspiring them and creating the conditions for them to flourish. So if there is an issue with them, take responsibility for it. Everyone will respect you a great deal more.

No one is indispensable.

Keep pruning the creative department so that it grows back healthier. No one is ever indispensable. Look at it as an opportunity to bring in new blood that will freshen up the department and create competition.

There are two types of creative that you should never keep around. Creative departments are often home to provocative and challenging characters. Good creative people in general are always looking to question the status quo, upending old thinking and ways of doing things, and this is exactly what you should want and encourage, as long as it is productive and they are doing it for the good of the work. When it strays outside the work and starts to cause division or upset, however, you need to deal with it. Sooner or later you will come across a wrong 'un in the creative department, someone who – for whatever reason – is toxic. I don't mean someone who has previously been a decent, functioning member of the team and who is going through a difficult time and taking it out on their mates; they need your support and understanding. I mean that person who is determined to cause collateral damage to morale. They need to go as quickly as possible, before they get a chance to build up a fan club and undermine the culture that everyone has bought into.

The other creatives you need to move on are the work-shy ones. They might be the most charming and beloved people in the department, but they are adding to the pressure and workload of the others. If the rest of the department can see that they aren't pulling their weight, this will cause resentment and affect productivity, regardless of how nice they are. You will be judged by the department and the agency at large for the type of people you are willing to tolerate, so be decisive and unsentimental. Agencies move on quickly.

The more talented people are, in my experience, the less they default to BEHAVING BADLY.

Helen Andrews
CEO, Johannes Leonardo NY

A door to close and a chair to plop down on and a place to stare at the wall or freely speak about what you're doing is like gold. **THEY DIDN'T WRITE *THE SOPRANOS* IN AN AIRPORT LOUNGE,** they have a writers' room for a reason.

Chris Beresford-Hill
Global CCO, BBDO

The creative space.

I've seen all kinds of approach to creative departments over the years: spreading creatives out across the agency to infuse the wider group with their creative passion; spreading creatives out across the agency to stop the creatives thinking they are special; having a fortress mentality where other departments fear to tread. Offices, booths, sheds and open-plan layouts in every permutation have come and gone as fashions change. Hybrid working is also now commonplace.

The only arrangements that I've ever seen actually work are those in which the creatives have space and quiet to think. That's how their best work gets done. The creative rhythm isn't like that of any other department. Planning comes closest, and I often thought planning and creative departments could coexist very happily. But a creative department that is quiet and messy is a happy, busy department. It takes a long time to get to the perfect flow state in which the best creative thinking is done, and it's achieved only through long periods of uninterrupted, focused concentration. Unfortunately, in open-plan environments it's next to impossible to get there because of the constant interruption, so people are forced to find sanctuary in their headphones or elsewhere.

Offices may not be in vogue right now, but they are productive, and every creative would be in one for choice. If you don't have offices, do whatever you can to make the surroundings suitable. Your department will love you for it. Bustling, open-plan, collaborative, creative spaces have a place in the life cycle of a project and can be used to great effect in the generation and review of creative ideas. That generally accounts for a small percentage of the overall creative development time, however, so it shouldn't take precedence. If the teams are constantly disappearing to find other places to work, it might be worth having a think about why.

6
Clients.
Love them
or lose them.

One of the quickest ways to lose a client is to treat them like a client. By that, I mean have a functional, transactional relationship with them. Our business is to help them to sell more of their products or services, and that's what they are paying for. But, fortunately, the very best clients also know brilliant creative work is their best chance of that happening. And that their best chance of getting to brilliant creative work is to have a strong and positive relationship with you, so that you will go above and beyond for them every time.

Such clients are rare, as you will know by now, and they tend to gravitate towards the best creative agencies and regularly get the best work, because they are smart and ambitious and want to make a name for themselves. If you are in one of those agencies, and these sound like most of your clients, you're off to a great start. They have come to that agency specifically to get good work, and in most cases are willing partners in what it takes to get to good work. If you're not in that agency with those clients – and this will apply to most of you – you're going to have to double down on your relationship with your clients and build the trust that will enable you both to get to better work. This takes time and effort on both sides, but it is worth it. Not just because you will get to better work, but also because you will create a much more enjoyable working environment for everyone involved. Any account where the CD and CMO like and respect each other is a real pleasure to be involved in.

In the interests of keeping this book as real-world as possible, I must also talk about the third type of client. Some clients, for whatever reason, just want a master–servant relationship instead of a partnership. You won't persuade them otherwise. They genuinely think that by bullying you and the agency they will get more out of you. (They won't, as anyone agency-side knows, but they will never see it that way.) Perhaps they are just dysfunctional people or working in a nasty 'shit-down' culture themselves. They will never do good work, and you will never build a relationship with them to get to good work. The more you try to do either, the further away you will end up.

Despite stories to the contrary, these clients are thankfully in the minority. If you're unlucky enough to get stuck with one of them, try not to take it personally. If, after you've tried everything in this chapter, nothing changes, the problem really is them and not you. Don't let them eat away at you. I have in the past, believing that it must have been something I said or did and that I should just try harder, only to hear that the same patterns emerged with other agencies they worked with. Don't give them any more energy than is necessary, and certainly don't waste any emotional energy. Smile. Do the job. Give them what they ask for. Be professional. Move on. Or they will drain you and your team of enthusiasm and confidence. If you are in the fortunate position of being able to afford to fire them, fire them. Because they won't just demotivate you, they will spread their toxic management skills throughout your team and affect your culture.

Anyway, enough energy on them. What follows is about building relationships with the vast majority of great clients who are out there, who are as desperate as you are to build a respectful partnership and do great things together. Good clients are the single biggest difference between having a great career and having an ordinary one. Some of my ex-clients are still good friends years later, because the relationship was genuine. They knew that I really wanted to do brilliant work, and would work with them to achieve it.

If I didn't have a strong relationship with a client, I would need to spend a month working on decks to convince them to do something. And the barrier is then higher because expectation rises, **THEY'RE NERVOUS, YOU'RE NERVOUS.** It's the wrong conditions.

Rodrigo Sobral
Global CCO, Oliver

Walk in their shoes.

Look at the world from the client's perspective, just as you would if you were trying to understand a consumer you wanted to target. This will help you to position your approach. What is going on in their day? What is keeping them up at night? What is the culture in their organisation? Do they get on with their boss? Does their team respect them?

The role of CMO and other senior client positions is incredibly tough. They are under immense pressure today as their remit expands constantly with more and more options appearing for their brand to exist in. They are drowning in data, have too many relationships to manage, struggle to have a strong voice at board level, and have to prove that what they are spending is driving a return or awareness or both. They are also constantly hit on by everyone trying to upsell them on something or get more budget for something else. And, by the way, what you do is only one of their responsibilities. They are a much bigger figure in your life than you are in theirs. But you are still extremely important to them. They need to feel that they can turn to you when they are feeling the pressure, and that will happen only if they feel that you understand the context they are operating in.

It's also important to remember that they are rarely the ultimate decision-makers in their organisation. They have a boss too, and in most cases, that boss isn't interested in how clever and creative the work you're doing is; they just want to know what the return on the investment will be. Your client wants to look good in front of their boss. I would always offer to go to the exco or board meetings when one of my clients was due to present an important new campaign. More often than not they were delighted for me to present and to have someone to share the responsibility with.

What would have made you stand out as a phenomenal creative can make YOU LOOK TERRIBLY NAIVE AS A CREATIVE LEADER. That's because you go from 'We want you to have the boldly ambitious radical creative idea' to a place where we still really need you to be selling the boldly ambitious radical creative idea, but you need to be able to do that with an understanding of why it's right for the client's business. To do that you need to know why it's right for their brief, so it raises the bar for great work because you have to be cognisant of and articulate in the sell beyond 'It's cool, it's great, it's bold, no one's done it before.'

Katie Mackay-Sinclair
Partner, Mother London

Clients are just regular people. They're not MING THE MERCILESS. They go home and they've got kids, and they go for a bike ride, or they go and watch GRIMSBY TOWN or they do the decorating.

Kevin Chesters
CSO, KC Consulting

Get to know them.

If walking in their shoes is about understanding them professionally, this is about getting to know them personally. Try showing a genuine interest in them, as you would when you meet anyone new. It doesn't have to be deep, and you don't have to be each other's BFFs, but it must be authentic. Just chat – you'll soon find shared interests. You might both come from the same town, support the same football team, love horse racing, knit, paint, love the films of Jean-Luc Godard. More unites us than divides us. Connections and interests outside work change the dynamic of the relationship and will remind you both that you are just two decent people doing their best to do a good job. It also gives you useful shared reference points.

  They are used to everyone wanting to be their friend, laughing at all their jokes or constantly affirming them, and if they are experienced they will probably be quite cynical about it. They know that it is because they control a budget that is the lifeblood of lots of agency people. But they are only human. Everyone wants to be liked, and if your attempts to get to know them are genuine they will respond. (Small, thoughtful things matter far more than grand gestures.) If they choose not to, you've lost nothing. The worst that can happen is that they think you are a friendly, empathetic person.

  The more open you are able to be about yourself, the warmer the relationship will be. Psychological studies prove that we want to spend time with people we like, and with people like us. Building this type of client relationship has long been seen as account management's responsibility, as historically creatives rarely spent much time with clients. Stop thinking of it as a responsibility; it's an opportunity.

Updates.

You're looking to foster trust and understanding, and one of the best ways to do that is through regular communication. When everyone is busy focusing on getting work done, it often happens that communication falls by the wayside. Keeping clients updated about the progress of their projects is a simple thing to do, but it's rarely done by the creative director. You are the one responsible for the work and immersed in its development, so hearing it from you makes a big difference. It's reassuring, and it makes for a calm and happy client.

It doesn't always have to be good news, either. I would often share some of the challenges I was coming up against, and I would also tell them if it was running later than expected because I wasn't happy with where we were. I never once had a bad response to this. Clients would appreciate that I was trying hard on their behalf to do a great job and not just letting anything through. Any update is better than no update, because in the absence of information it's easy for a client to imagine the worst and carry that escalating anxiety into the presentation. As well as reassuring clients about your progress, regularly reaching out to them demonstrates that their business is at the top of your mind and has your attention.

A little watch-out, however. Opening a personal line of communication with your client says that they matter to you, but don't allow it to creep into your personal time. On the odd occasion and at high-pressure moments, out-of-hours communication goes with the job territory, so you'll just need to suck it up. But if it becomes a regular thing, politely set clear time boundaries. I've had many instances over the years of a client calling me on a Sunday morning and saying, 'I was thinking ...', or texting at six in the morning expecting an immediate response. It may show that your opinion is important to them, but it's not something you should encourage.

The client needs to know that if they have any concerns, they can just say: 'CAN WE TALK?' And a creative director needs to be able to do that comfortably. Sometimes badly trained creatives almost see a client as the obstacle to getting to great work. They're the gateway.

**Charlie Rudd
CEO, Creative Practice, Publicis Groupe UK**

If you're feeling awkward, you make clients feel awkward. And then they don't believe that you have the answer. Clients fundamentally don't believe that you have the answer or that you'll get to the answer. Or that you have the authority to tell them what the answer is. Because that's what they're really looking for from you. **THEY WANT TO KNOW THAT YOU BELIEVE IT.** And that you'll get there. They need to believe you that you'll get it right.

Nicholas Hulley
Joint CCO, AMV BBDO London

Calm and confident.

Yes, I know you've put your heart and soul into it, it matters to the whole agency, it's account-critical, the temperature is rising. Expectations are sky-high. This work could be famous, could start an awards rush, a new business run, attract the best talent, make your name. But the last thing you should be doing is putting all that pressure on display around a client. Getting sweaty and uptight will not increase your chances of the client buying it from you.

I hate being presented to by nervous people – it makes me nervous. That's because we all feed off confidence. In behavioural science, it's called the Messenger Effect. The more authoritative and in control the speaker appears, the surer we are that we can trust what they are telling us. It's why influencers and testimonials are so powerful.

So, avoid the build-up becoming pressurised. Take the heat out of it by seeding in the thinking to the client as early as possible, unofficially. No one wants to be put on the spot, and you rarely get the best from anyone when you do that. Informal chats, ideally one on one, yield the best results. Give them a chance to hear a suggestion of what it might be in an unpressured environment, perhaps over a coffee or at the chatty back-end of another meeting. Don't go into details, just float the premise.

Most of the best work I did as a creative director came about in this way. It allows your client to come into a presentation with an understanding of what they will see. They have had time to validate it for themselves and quite possibly sell it along their own line of command. They will also recognise their comments from your chat and feel a co-ownership. Then, when it comes to the big presentation, you can really enjoy it and make it enjoyable for everyone else because you know the audience is going to applaud. Happy you. Happy client.

Active listening.

You know when you're at a party or a dinner and you're sitting next to someone who talks about themselves relentlessly? Exactly. Incredibly boring, isn't it? You wonder to yourself, how on earth can they be so self-absorbed and lacking in awareness that they assume you're enjoying it, when, in fact, you're just waiting for the first polite opportunity to move away? Make sure this isn't you. It's easy to be that person when you're keen to impress upon your new client what you can do for them, what you have done for other clients, what great work you're known for, all the awards you've won, how excited you are for the challenge of their brand, etc. You think you're being keen and enthusiastic and full of excited energy; they think you're a self-absorbed bore and are wondering if they can get away with inventing a 'hard stop' to the meeting.

At the heart of any good business relationship is active listening. This means giving someone your undivided attention, listening to their challenges, thoughts and concerns, not just waiting for them to stop talking so that you can talk.

So, before you charge in and dominate the presentation or meeting by offloading weeks of built-up anxiety about the work and what you want to achieve with it, stop and listen. Give your client the opportunity to talk first. They may even say something that gives you insight into what they are looking for or hoping to see from you. Take a few notes as they speak and refer to them when it's your turn to talk; this will help you tailor your narrative to one that will ease the process of getting the work bought into. Listen more than you talk. It will make what you do say more valuable and impactful.

Under-promise and over-deliver.

Over-delivering is almost certainly something you do anyway. That's why you're in a creative leadership role. You know that every client interaction matters, and that the client hopes to see some magic every time they meet you, so don't disappoint them. That's a lot easier to do if you're careful to manage their expectations first.

Expectations, as we've discussed at length in Chapter 4, are just premeditated disappointments. And hype has a horrible habit of backfiring. Never big up what you're doing or planning to show, or make the promise of the meeting being more amazing than you'll be able to deliver on, just because you're nervous and you want them to like you. Regardless of how good it is, it won't be as good as they now expect. Far better that a client comes in with lowered expectations. They'll like you well enough if you impress them in the meeting, so hold your nerve. 'It's amazing – it will break the internet' is the prelude to a terrible meeting. It also suggests a hubris on your part that is never quite as beguiling as you think. Better to talk about it as 'delivering against the brief', 'showing signs of promise', or something similarly reassuring and understated.

Then, when it's time to present, do so with real passion and enthusiasm for the work, and make sure that every presentation goes further than the client was expecting. Maybe it's taking the execution further than you'd promised, or perhaps you've brought along music suggestions to bring in some unexpected emotion, or a new route that you're excited by, or even how the idea stretches into a new and interesting technology. Whatever it is, it's invaluable because it shows that you're committed enough to do it, and that you're not just doing what you're being paid to do. Being professional is table stakes for a creative director. Being amazing should be your ambition.

Taking feedback.

This is one of the flashpoint moments that can make or break a CD–client relationship. And once broken, there is rarely a chance of repairing it. I always bristled silently at client feedback on a shoot, mostly because nine times out of ten, it wasn't real feedback, it was pure anxiety. That was understandable, since most shoots are high stakes for clients. But also, I was feeling the pressure of a situation that I wasn't totally in control of given the large number of variables, and I wanted to keep my full focus on delivering what I'd said I would. I had to take a few deep breaths, affect my most patient air, sit next to them in agency-village (the last place a CD should be on a shoot), and use up valuable time listening to their concerns and explaining what was actually happening and why it was going to be fine. If I couldn't reassure them, I would have to ask the director to shoot what they asked for so that we had it covered, knowing full well that it would be forgotten about by the time we were editing.

As much as this felt like precious time wasted, it was anything but. It was building the client's trust and respect for my knowledge and the craft of filmmaking. It also enabled the shoot to progress without a build-up of tension, which can eat away at everyone. The couple of times I didn't do this and just snapped back with a dismissive response, I regretted it the second it came out of my mouth, and – unsurprisingly – it didn't end well for me or the work.

The truth is, the way you respond to client feedback determines how ardently they stick to it. If you give them three reasons why they are wrong before they've even finished speaking, it will descend into an argument that you'll lose. It doesn't matter how passionately you disagree. Listen. Pause. Reflect. Respond. And if you can't think of anything constructive to say, buy yourself some thinking and calming-down time by saying you want to think it through and get back to them. You'll be very glad you did.

There's always extreme uncertainty [with creative development], which makes people stressed out. So, when a client gives feedback or voices their concerns, **REPEAT IT BACK TO THEM** to make sure they have actually heard you, saying, 'I heard you say you're worried about this being too dark. I hear you.' They will relax. Then you can move forward.

Felix Richter
CCO, Mother London

Take a hit.

Deliberately allow a piece of work to go out that you don't particularly like or that isn't as good as it could be. What?!? This might seem counter-intuitive and against the sacred code of the creative director, but it has a time and place in every good CD–CMO relationship. Every so often I made work that I hated, because a client reached out for my help. For the record, I would make it clear that I didn't like it, and why. But I would say it with a smile and make the process as easy for them as possible, because I knew they were asking for it to alleviate the extreme pressure they were under.

For example, I was asked by an otherwise great client to do a series of terrible posters that appeared along the main road from Heathrow airport to their UK HQ in central London, so that their global CEO would see them when he visited. The headlines and visual were something he had suggested in a previous meeting and made him feel listened to, which went some way towards rebuilding my client's fractious relationship with Global. My work on this was always met with a thank-you for my understanding and the acknowledgement that it gave me something in the bank to draw on when I needed it.

The reality is that if a client needs something like that done, it will happen whether you like it or not. So to make it hard for them when they are already feeling awkward about asking is self-sabotage. Make it easy and pleasant, and they will feel they are in a trusting partnership. If it happens with regularity, however, you have a different problem. This is one to discuss with your leadership team, because the issue will require a more serious conversation with your client to understand what is driving it.

Always save your battles for the big stuff. That way you will be listened to when it's your turn to ask for a favour. No one takes any notice of the little dog that yaps constantly.

Never ignore junior clients.

There are several reasons for not ignoring the junior clients and focusing your attention on the most senior person in the room. First among them is that junior clients grow up into senior clients quite quickly, and they don't forget how they were made to feel. People in marketing have the shortest average job tenure of any industry. So within a year or two there's a good chance they will be promoted to a senior role or be running another brand and keen to work with you again.

Another reason for bothering with junior clients is that most people don't, and they will appreciate the extra effort you're putting in. Especially if you take the time and trouble to include them in the conversation so that their only chance to speak isn't that awkward bit at the end of a meeting when the senior client asks for their opinion. Don't underestimate the influence of junior clients within their organisation, particularly if they are rising stars. Having them speaking well of you and your influence on their business can be the difference between you getting work through and not.

Finally, a good senior client wants their juniors to have the confidence to take up some of the slack. For this reason, they will be extremely grateful to see you being active in their juniors' education and giving them your support.

As you gain experience as a creative leader, mentoring more junior members of the team – whether they are agency or client side – will become almost second nature. You will start to enjoy sharing your knowledge and seeing others benefit from it. Putting a junior member in their place just because you can is the surest way to lose everyone's respect, and the account. So, if at first it strikes you as a bit cynical to bother with junior clients, remember that everyone will benefit from it in the long run.

The c-word.

Like all good behavioural nudges, this simple hint takes next to no effort and makes a disproportionate difference. Stop calling the client 'The Client' internally. Creative hackles go up the moment the word 'client' is used. It's so loaded, and it immediately conjures unwanted images of some perceived injustice or engenders a combative response. It shouldn't – that's unprofessional – but too often it does. It's really not helpful in building enthusiasm for their account, and it'll come back to bite you. If your team don't think you like or respect a client, they're unlikely to give it their all. You need to change the narrative regardless of your own personal feelings, because you set the tone for how you expect everyone to behave. If you look up the meaning of the word, it's clear and unambiguous: *In business, a client is a type of customer who buys professional services.* They are paying for a professional service and have every right to expect to be valued.

We're in a human capital business, and we pride ourselves on being able to connect with people through our understanding of their unmet needs, yet we often dehumanise one of the most important relationships we have. So just call them by their first name. 'Tom called with some feedback.' 'Emily is coming in tomorrow to discuss production.' When you use the client's name, you're telling your teams that you like and respect this person. The more you refer to them by name, the more others will, and the more the barriers will start to come down. You want clients to enjoy their interaction with the agency, to feel at home when they visit. This will help.

I once heard a very well-known and successful creative say: 'HOW CAN I WRITE AN AD FOR A CLIENT IF YOU TELL ME THE CLIENT'S SHIT? Only ever talk to me about the client in a way that I can like them.'

Tanya Livesey
Global MD Creative & Design, TTB

7
How to master pitching.

Imagine going for a meal. You book four restaurants. You eat at all of them over the course of a week. Four amazing meals, with drinks, and you don't pay for any of them. The restaurants, however, still have to pay the wages of the staff who prepared and served those meals. They still have to pay for the ingredients that went into the meals, and for the drinks. They also had to give up a table that would have gone to someone who was paying for their meal. You then call three of the restaurants back a week or two later and tell them why the meal they prepared didn't really do it for you. The restaurants thank you for considering them in the first place. You then call the restaurant that made your preferred meal, tell them that the meal was OK, but needs work, and offer to pay them less than they wanted for it. In return, you promise to continue to eat there for the foreseeable future, although you can't guarantee that you will only eat there or that you will continue to do so for longer than thirty days if you go off them at any point.

If restaurants offered this as an option, we would all take them up on it. But there's a very good reason why they don't. And neither do lawyers, surgeons, plumbers, mechanics, accountants … in fact, no one does it except us. It's a disastrous economic model. But whenever agencies willingly enter into the pitching process, clients will take advantage of it. And in an over-subscribed industry (there are 17,720 UK creative agencies at the time of writing), that is unlikely to change. The average agency cost of a pitch in the UK is currently £50,000 and comes with only a 1 in 3 chance of a return.* The average number of pitches an agency does in a year is 11, so that's £550,000 of pitch costs annually. That means the UK advertising industry has to soak up £9.75 billion in pitch costs every year. And it's growing.

I perfectly understand the reason for pitches. This is a people business. Clients want to see that you are a cultural fit for them, that you have the skills they need, and that you get along. But you don't need a full-blown creative pitch to find that out. A chemistry session and talking through client case studies with creative work

---

*www.campaignlive.co.uk/article/average-pitch-cost-rises-26-agencies-target-fewer-bigger-better-reviews/1887290

would achieve that. Every time you pitch you are giving away a lot of time, money, energy, resource, valuable thinking and goodwill. So if you are going to pitch you must make it as painless as possible. You should also be sure to retain the intellectual property of any work you present, so that it can't be used at a later date for free. A good client will be happy to agree to this.

So you've decided to pitch. You want the account enough to invest in trying to win it. You've driven everyone around you into the ground for the last month or so to deliver a world-class solution, and you're running on fumes yourself. The day of the pitch arrives. Adrenalin, coffee and last night's cold pizza are flying around in your exhausted and jittery system, which is making your skin itch. You've got all the work in place with only moments to spare, and it's too late to change the typo that has just been helpfully pointed out to you. You didn't have time to write presentation notes. Shit. Shit. Shit. You've thanked, promised undying love for, and hugged everyone you've spent the last 72 selfless hours straight with, and texted your wife/husband/partner yet another apology without getting a reply. You've smiled warmly, shaken the hands of the straight-faced clients as they've filed in, introduced yourself and already forgotten their names. You've done your best to make it look as though the agency team are quite literally your best mates with some awkward matey banter. You've actively listened and nodded as the planner bangs on and on, spotted another typo, realised that you urgently need a pee, then suddenly the entire room falls silent and looks at you.

You're up. This is the big moment, the bit everyone has really come to see. The last month is dancing on this pinhead. You're expected to present every last piece of work faultlessly and passionately, setting it in the context of the strategy and business need, dazzling everyone with your urbane wit, and displaying a warm humility that will overcome people's preconceptions of how difficult creative directors are. You then take a series of deliberately tricky questions from the anxious and uptight clients, while being judged ruthlessly by everyone in the room, including your own agency team. And by the way, if you are anything less than charming, you've blown it. All of it. And you'll have to explain why to the twenty people who worked on the pitch behind the scenes, around the clock, for the last four weeks. You OK with that? No. Of course you're not – no one is. But, give or take, this is a typical pitch experience.

So how do you make that an atypical experience? How do you make pitches absolutely brilliant and life-affirming, and become a serial winner? I've no idea. But don't worry, no one does. Of course, agencies have golden periods, when their stock is so high that pitching becomes like shooting fish in a barrel, but they are the minority. What I can tell you, though, is how to make pitching less stressful and less wasteful of time and resource, how to increase your chances of winning, how to still be talking to everyone by the end of it, and how not to annoy all your existing clients.

Are you the right person for it?

Are you the best casting for the pitch? If you're the most senior creative leader in the business, there is an assumption that you'll be doing it. But you know what we say about assumptions. You may not have any option, in which case you are definitely the right person for the pitch. But if there are other possibilities, consider them. You don't have to lead every pitch.

Don't allow your decision to be driven by insecurity. A strong creative leader will always be happy to mentor another creative director or senior creative, and there are a bunch of reasons why this is a good idea. To begin with, it could be that they are a better fit for the sector or brand, perhaps because they have useful experience in that area. First-hand knowledge of a sector or a brand is invaluable, particularly if the pitch has a short timeline. Understanding the pitfalls and clichés of a sector will save you a lot of time and trouble and reassure the clients that you 'get' them. It may just be that it's a sector that they have a personal interest in or are an avid consumer of. In that case they'll bring real passion to the project.

Second, pitching offers career progression to up-and-coming talent, and anyone who is ambitious will jump at it. Be really clear with them that you are mentoring them through the process, but that their decision on the work is final. This avoids the pitch team trying to work around them to get to you if they aren't confident in the work. You are there to advise the creative director running the pitch, not run the pitch yourself. You can always be in the pitch on the day to introduce the team and offer back-up if necessary.

Third, if you are pitching frequently, you are neglecting your day job. Pitches can become very draining, both emotionally and creatively. You can't afford to be missing in action for extended periods and affect the momentum of your accounts or the agency generally.

Team chemistry and roles.

If the team don't get on for whatever reason, it's amplified in the room. And that's game over. What client would entrust their account, their chances of success and ultimately their job to a bunch of jokers who clearly don't have any chemistry? The team needs a balance of characters, but it also needs absolute clarity on roles or there will be clashes. For that to happen there must be trust and respect. If you can't manage that, don't pitch – you won't win.

The nucleus of any pitch team is the creative director and the planner to drive the thinking, the business director to challenge and build on that thinking with a particular emphasis on the business need, and the PM to drive logistics. Clear roles. Clear responsibilities. The planner who thinks they're a creative, or the account person who thinks they're a planner, wastes time and energy and never improves the output. There's a time and a place for unsolicited opinions, and it's not during a pitch. Everyone else involved in the pitch should be additive: to build out the creative work, to refine the support points and so on. All focused on the same target. Make sure your team compliments each other and are easy in each other's company.

Watch out for the 'Problem Spotter'. They are the ones who have a problem for every solution. They're not to be confused with strong characters who are willing to challenge you, as those people typically build on the thinking. No, these guys are the under-confident power players who want the room to think theirs is the view that matters most. They don't really have anything useful to add, and they certainly never table any brilliant and original thinking. They prefer to create tension, and they're the masters of insinuating that they are the keepers of the key to unlock the pitch. They aren't. You are. Most are quite senior, so they won't be easy to weed out, but do your best to bench them.

Do your homework.

Preparation. Preparation. Preparation. What is driving their need to pitch? Where has their team worked before? What work have they bought in the past? Have they written any articles that you could reference? Do you know anyone in common? Do they have any advice? What financial shape is their business in? What are the big narratives in their sector? Are they successful or on the back foot?

You get the idea. The more you know about a potential client, the easier it will be for you to shape an appropriate response. It's a very rare pitch that is called solely because they want to see better creative work, despite what the client or pitch consultant may say. Mostly it's a breakdown of a relationship, a build-up of friction, a new CMO wanting people loyal to them, or a need to negotiate costs. And everyone on the client side in the pitch room will be coming to it looking for you to solve the issues as they see them. There is absolutely no point putting a brilliantly creative pitch together if it doesn't answer their needs, so find out what those needs are.

Understanding the world they are operating in will also give you a better idea of their pain points regarding agency relationships. Being able to demonstrate that you are able to alleviate them in your approach will give you a head start.

Clients are as nervous as you are. A lot is riding on this pitch. Often, their jobs. The choice and subsequent success or failure of their new partner will have a huge impact on their standing within their own organisation.

You should also do your homework on the individuals in the room. That will not only offer insight into the decision-makers, but also give you plenty of conversation-starters. Discovering shared interests always comes in useful, because in pitches people buy people, particularly those who show that they are willing to go over and above to understand them and their organisation.

Tell them what you're going to say. Say it. Then tell them what you said.

I learned a valuable lesson many years ago during a screenwriting course I took at Birkbeck College. We were told to write a scene with three characters in it. We were then told to halve the dialogue. It was amazing how easily we could all strip away unnecessary words. We were then told to halve it again. This was harder. But eventually, we all had taut scenes that were focused and clear. And every word mattered.

You can guess where I'm going with this. Most pitches don't fail because the thinking isn't first class. They fail because the client didn't realise the thinking was first class, and that was simply because they were overwhelmed by all the talking and couldn't get a grip on what they were being told. We all cram so much new and interesting information into a pitch that it's impossible for everything to land. And, because we're running at speed to get it done in time, we rarely allow time to sit with the presentation and edit. Then edit again. And again, until the presentation contains only what it needs to land in the time allowed.

Timed run-throughs only compound matters. The focus of run-throughs is to make sure the logic flow works, the handovers are smooth and every slide can be presented in the time. But by then you all know the work and the thinking. You've lived with it for weeks. You are not thinking about whether it'll be a mental overload for the audience. You might be able to say it in the time, but will they be able to take it all in?

So, halve your dialogue, then halve it again. Focus on the key point. Give yourself the time to tell them what they are going to see and why. Then show it to them. Allow them to feel it. Then summarise what you just showed them. If the creative idea and the reasoning for it don't land clearly, the last few weeks have all been wasted.

The amount of money that gets invested, in terms of both staff time and third-party costs, means that unless you can hang on to that client for at least two or three years at full profitability, full margin, YOU'LL NEVER GET IT BACK.

David Spencer
CFO, Goodby Silverstein & Partners SF

Go wide, then go deep.

Pitches eat up resource that could be put on to existing clients' work. And resource is always tight. So, use teams efficiently. Don't allow a pitch to impact the entire department, unless it is the mother of all pitches and will change the fortunes of the agency forever.

My approach was to start with a handful of teams, as many as I could spare for a couple of days. When there are a number of teams, no one will feel they own it, and that generally means they will be more fearless in their responses, which is a great way to kick off. Ask them to generate lots of thoughts, then review as a group and pull out anything that is even vaguely interesting. Get everyone to see what everyone is doing and encourage them all to build on the thoughts. This is a fantastic multiplier of ideas and generates a lot of fun and energy. It's also a great well of ideas that you can keep drawing from throughout the process, and it'll show you where the heat is for certain creative areas, which is often a useful yardstick.

Be sure to keep your CSO in these meetings. Not especially for their creative builds, but it saves a huge amount of time on catch-up meetings and keeps them really connected to your thinking. Good planners will also chip in with builds to strengthen the links back to the brief and prompts to cover areas that have been missed. This approach also fosters a sense of unity.

Now cut the group down to the fewest teams possible who seem to get the brief the best, and go again. Make it clear to them that the work is now their responsibility, and free up everyone else to get back to their day jobs. If you do need a little more creative juice during the process, you'll have teams who already know what it's about.

It's easy to get carried away with a pitch. We all like to win. It's great for PR and internal energy. You get to show your creative genius unfettered by the demands of reality. But don't let it create resource problems for you on existing business.

Try not to write.

If you have to, you have to. But if you have the option not to, take it. Your responsibility on a pitch is to define the direction of travel, or even in some cases come up with the creative platform around which the pitch will be built. Then inspire, review and refine the creative work that expresses it most compellingly. It's close to impossible to stay objective when you are down in the detail writing executions. Of course, it's tempting and fun. If you have an absolute pitch winner of an execution, don't hold back. But as a rule, leave the ideation and execution to your department.

If you do write on a pitch, it's easy to get sucked into thinking that your ideas are great, particularly if they answer the brief neatly. Unfortunately, it's unlikely that anyone is going to tell you that they aren't great. It takes a brave soul to tell the creative director that their work is a bit, well, workmanlike. It hasn't had the benefit of going through a review process with someone as good as you to build on it with fresh eyes and nudge it into a better place. Everyone needs a creative director to get the best out of their work, particularly when they're under time pressure.

Consider too that the department was looking forward to writing on the pitch. It's fun writing on something that doesn't come with all the usual caveats and complications. All creatives love writing big ideas on something new, so let them enjoy it. Pitches can be great for morale if they are handled carefully.

Writing also eats up time that you don't have. Either you won't have the time to write it with the level of thought and craft you would expect of your teams, or you'll be using up time that would have a greater value spent elsewhere.

The most significant reason, though, is that writing on a pitch makes it almost impossible for you to see the bigger picture with clarity. If that happens, you'll struggle to build a compelling case for why the platform is right.

We made the absolute rookie mistake when we first became ECDs. We did a pitch, and we tried to do everything on the pitch ourselves. So we thought like a creative team rather than creative directors. Do the work, WRITE THE THEME TUNE, SING THE THEME TUNE, do everything. And of course, because you're so close and you don't have a wider view, it went wrong. Then, of course, we lost and it was quite a big bit of business. You have to reflect. I think it's absolutely fine to make a mistake once, but the real trick is not to make it again.

Alex Grieve
Global & London CCO, BBH

When I became a CD and was doing my first pitch, the account team told me what to wear. And they said, 'Could you talk slower? Because you're A BIT TOO NORTHERN. Just make sure you pronounce your words.' I thought, fuck this, I went in and was just me. You've got to be who you are. And my strength is in excitement. Everybody's got to find their thing. Everyone can be great in meetings. They just need to feel confident. I go in, and I'm very animated, and I get very excited, and I'll start scribbling. What about this? That's my thing. We WON the pitch.

Richard Brim
Former CCO, Adam & Eve DDB London

You do you.

It's a massive cliché, but there's often a lot of truth in massive clichés: Be the best version of you.

I don't do jazz hands. I'm considered. I speak slowly and softly, pause a lot and laugh at my own jokes, but all this has served me very well because it is true to me. Having the confidence to be yourself is a very powerful way to stay calm and get people to trust you. If ever I need a moment to gather my thoughts, I use my glasses as a prop to buy me a second or two. If I'm presenting, I'll stand up and walk around. That enables me to be more expressive and to stand closer to the person I'm addressing, to increase the sense of connection. I've also discovered that pausing works wonders for drawing people into a story.

I'm not suggesting for a moment that this is the right approach for you. You might be all high energy and drama, in which case stick with that. You need to experiment with what works for you. There's no right or wrong way. And don't listen to anyone who tries to change you. If you're relaxed, the room is relaxed.

Just make sure that your way is clear and engaging. Mumbling and grunting at the floor are not personal presentation styles. There is no shortage of presentation courses if you feel you need some help. But the key is to rehearse repeatedly. That will allow you to be the best, real, calm version of you. We all buy into warm and engaging people, not slick, polished performers.

There is one watch-out, however: talking too fast. Everyone does this at first without realising it. Your adrenaline is pumping, you're feeling the pressure, and you want to get it all out there. But remember that the clients are taking in a lot of important new information and need time to process it if they are to appreciate how good it is. If you're a fast talker, slow it down until it seems too slow. That will be the right pace to allow the audience to take it all in.

Great work doesn't always speak for itself.

Most creatives are on the introverted side of the spectrum. A natural and spontaneous public speaker and presenter is a rare talent in a creative department. The thought of standing up in front of a room of clients and making a reasoned yet impassioned case for why our pitch work was brilliant filled me with complete and utter dread early on in my career. I used to write last-minute notes and try to remember them, but it was a disaster every time. I'd dry up because I'd forgotten the notes, and then, worse than that, I'd read from my notes. It lost all the sincerity that I genuinely had.

    This problem arises because the creative director is typically the last to know what they are going to say in a pitch. Strategy was sorted long ago, so the planner has had time to prepare, and their slides are like prompts so they get to look smart. But you're still trying to get the art direction to work on the 87 pieces of creative that are going into the meeting. You haven't had a second to build a brilliant case for why you've done what you've done. And, despite what anyone says, it's always the creative work that wins or loses the pitch. Start thinking about your deck from the start. Plan your presentation early, even if it's just making notes along the way. So much great stuff is said en route to the presentation and forgotten. If you can memorise it, great. If you can't, have prompt slides built into the deck. But in both cases, rehearse.

    You aren't just presenting the work. Clients want to hear what you think: why you believe the work will be famous; why the work not only answers their needs but exceeds them; why the work will seize hold of the hearts of the nation and make their brand loved. They want to be inspired and beguiled by your confidence in the creative work. Never think that great work will sell itself in a pitch just by you reading it out. You have to organise your thinking long before you step into the room so that your case is as compelling as that of the best barrister.

We never built in time for pitch rehearsals, until we did presentation training with RADA. The guy training us asked about our rehearsal schedule. We were like, 'We don't rehearse. Normally we like it to have energy and spontaneity.' AND HE LOOKED AT US LIKE WE WERE IDIOTS and said, 'Do you ever go to the cinema?' Yeah, obviously! 'Do you go to the theatre?' Yeah, of course! 'Have you ever seen a band perform live?' Yeah! 'How often do you think they rehearse before you see them? How many times do you think they've done that scene before they get the perfect one? How many different ways do you think that cast on stage tried that dialogue? How many times do you think that band played that track? Did it feel any less spontaneous or special or magic?' And we were like, 'Wow, you really handed it to us there, didn't you?' I felt ashamed to think that us just off the cuff would be great. We expect so much more from other creative products that we pay handsomely for, and it changed my perspective ... It's really important, even if you don't have time, just walk through it and think of yourself as a performer.

Katie Mackay-Sinclair
Partner, Mother London

Be memorable.

Ideally for something good. Not for ripping £5,000 worth of plaster off a client's wall while taking down pitch work that had been put up with industrial-strength tape, as I once did. With the exception of destroying the client's boardroom, there's nothing worse than being forgettable. Pitch theatre is often used as a way to create memorability. But unless it is highly relevant and thoughtfully executed, it can go against you as often as it goes for you, leaving everyone feeling rather awkward. Far better that you consider doing or saying something with a little more substance.

The clients are seeing lots of people during the pitch process. They will be struggling to remember who said and did what. Of course, you should be remembered for the brilliant thinking that you sweated blood for. But, honestly, everybody else sweated blood for theirs, too. Everyone presented a great pitch. It's always possible that someone presented something laughably bad or misjudged and they'll be remembered for the wrong reasons, but you need to go over and above to be remembered for something more than just the brilliant work.

For clients under pressure, it has all mushed into a bit of a blur. It's incredibly hard for anyone to sit through three or four pitches over a couple of days and remember the killer points in all of them, process that information, form a reasoned conclusion, put it in the context of the personalities and cultures they met, and reach a firm decision as to which agency they should award their business to. It's a lot to take in, and everyone will have something smart and professional that is demanding of consideration.

As Maya Angelou famously said, 'People will remember how you made them feel, long after they've forgotten what you said to them.' What will your pitch be remembered for?

Questions and feedback.

There are few bigger moments of relief than finishing your creative presentation on a pitch. Weeks of graft, anxiety, lost sleep, hopes and dreams all culminate in this euphoric split second. You're spent and can do no more. You retake your seat, a victorious warrior sheathing your blade. The continuing voices blur into the background. You pour yourself a well-earned tea and help yourself to one of the posh pastries that were over-ordered. You're already thinking of meeting the pitch team in the pub to celebrate it being over, or going home, seeing the kids, taking a shower and going to sleep.

Big mistake. It's not over. Suddenly a difficult question about the work is fired at you. Like a reverse crash zoom, you are back in the room, gaping like a goldfish. Always be prepared for criticism or questioning. Keep your focus until the clients are in the lifts. How you answer is important. It will be remembered, because it's an indication of what you will be like to work with. I always optimistically took questions as a good sign and was happy to answer them, no matter how tricky they were. My reasoning was that if the clients weren't interested in the work or in us, why would they bother asking questions about it or critiquing it?

Don't rush into answering. Pause. Gather yourself and stay calm. Praise them for their question or observation. Whatever you do, don't get flustered. If you don't know the answer to the question, don't start waffling, say you don't know and that you will follow up with them. It's always better to offer a decisive response. This will also give you a fantastic opportunity to re-present the key points of the pitch in your follow-up email.

The pitch is never over until it's over. And those pastries always taste better when the clients have left the room.

8
Inspiring a creative culture across the agency.

'A Creative Culture' is one of those overused phrases that everyone nods along to without being entirely sure what it means in practice. Do you know what it means in practice? You're not alone. A large percentage of creative people in advertising and communications don't either. I didn't for many years. The confusion comes from how the industry has traditionally defined creativity.

Creativity in the world of advertising and communications referred only to the creative work, by which I mean the executional output, and people who had 'creative' in their job title were the sole custodians of it. This narrow definition of creativity was the cornerstone of the industry. It proved highly successful for many years, and while there were a limited number of clearly defined and well-understood creative deliverables, there was no burning desire to challenge it. So, a creative culture meant somewhere that was dominated by the creative department; everyone else was there as an ancillary service. Nice and straightforward. It continues to this day in a number of excellent businesses that tend to be built around the cult of a particular creative leader or, in most cases, creative founder, and focus on a limited range of deliverables, typically high-value brand assets. If everyone involved buys into that culture, it can still be extremely powerful.

But, as I'm sure you've noticed, the world has changed and the problems we are asked to solve have grown more complex, requiring a much faster response by a broader mix of skill sets, necessitating seamless connectivity. Consequently, the need for creative thinking has grown dramatically in every direction, leading to a far more expansive definition of creativity as the single most powerful business and life skill you can possess, and one that is fundamental to everyone's role within the business. This view is endorsed by the World Economic Forum, which considers creativity to be essential if individuals and businesses are to prosper at a time of accelerated change. Creativity is now being championed for its ability to transform the world for the better, drive global innovation and progress, encourage resilience and embrace change in a fast-changing world. This is a far more useful and future-facing definition for anyone responsible for running a creative business, but it does have a sizable impact on how a business is run.

Without question, you will arrest your agency's development if you make creativity the sole domain of your creative department. They are the experts in bringing an idea to life, of creative execution, but not of creativity in general. There is a clear separation between the two. The more expansive definition of creativity, the one that encourages creativity in everyone, still leads to great creative output and does nothing to diminish the importance of creative craft, but it takes a broader view of how to get there, who is involved and what the output might be. It celebrates specialists and promotes collaboration. By cordoning off creativity like a crime scene, you miss the rich, diverse perspectives and ideas that lie dormant across other departments. Innovative thinking should be encouraged to flourish in every department of the agency.

When a business fosters an inclusive creative working environment, the collective brainpower increases your ability to adapt to the constant demands of change and enables you to apply your collective creativity in many more ways. It stops the formation of silos that become set in their ways and uncompetitive. It will also create a far more enjoyable working environment that leads to fewer tension points, politics and factions. The other upside, of course, is that those employees are more productive and stay longer because morale is higher and they believe in the agency's values. No department has the monopoly on creative thinking. Creative execution, yes, but not creative thinking. The more every department feels encouraged to think in creative and innovative ways, the more limitless your team's creative potential will feel.

You will need to be active in encouraging a commitment to creativity across the business; it won't just happen of its own accord. For you, the creative director, to be the champion of it is a very powerful statement that you are serious about inclusivity and building a truly creative culture. Make sure you regularly seek out new ideas from different people. Encourage them. Reward them. Celebrate them.

It's a role that demands much more partnership and camaraderie and understanding than perhaps the **CLICHÉD STEREOTYPE OF THE ISOLATIONIST, SOMETIMES AGGRESSIVE, ALPHA CREATIVE DIRECTOR.** That doesn't mean that I wouldn't also want them to be fiercely opinionated and have a really clear sense of where we're headed, but they need to be able to take people with them. I think the taking people with you has become more and more important as time has gone on, because we have to convince more people now to take risks in a volatile environment, where there's much more pressure. To be a creative leader you have to be able to hold that tension between 'I know where we need to get to' and 'I also know how to make sure everyone feels heard and comes along on the journey.'

**Katie Mackay-Sinclair
Partner, Mother London**

You want to be able to speak freely, without judgement or fear of judgement around work. The best creative leaders I've worked or partnered with **CREATE A CULTURE OF CURIOSITY**. People join this industry, no matter what their discipline, if they have a natural curiosity about creativity, about taste, about things in culture. The more you can allow a culture of curiosity to bring stimulus into that discussion, the better.

Bill Scott
CEO, Droga5 London

Encourage collaborative creativity.

Committing to creativity across the business is the first step in creating a truly creative culture. Encouraging collaborative creativity is the second. Often, creatives are reluctant to collaborate with other departments. They feel that they are trained creative professionals and resent the intrusion. In truth, when they are developing work using their craft skills, such collaboration is rarely helpful. But at all other times, collaboration in whatever form it takes is a creative accelerator. Don't just look at it from the creative department's point of view, either. By encouraging collaborative creativity when it is most useful, you are making creative thinking intrinsic to your culture. Collaborative creativity works best when team members have different experiences, skills and perspectives. It can create unique and challenging (in a positive way) fusions.

There is also a modern reality to the work that agencies are engaged in. It covers so many touchpoints, with so many different needs to communicate successfully, that no one knows enough on their own. As the complexity of problems increases sharply, so the need for collaborative creativity will expand. Never allow the creative department to become a fortress that repels incomers; those days are over for a reason. Collaborative creativity also has a virtuous circular benefit. Its social nature encourages an increase in positive social relationships between departments, and a wealth of research indicates that teams whose members like one another and get on tend to produce more creative and innovative ideas.

However, you do need to make sure the ground rules are set to avoid it turning into a free-for-all. Fortunately, that is relatively straightforward as long as you are clear about who owns what stage and who is there in support. Collaborative creativity falls apart with collaborative responsibility.

Allow some chaos.

Rules can be important when they are used to reinforce positive behaviours, but enforcing rules for their own sake will only constrict creativity. To have a creative culture, an organisation must embrace the messy freedoms necessary for creative minds across the business to thrive.

If you want talented people to consistently deliver brilliantly creative responses to the challenges they are set, regardless of what department they are in, give them the freedom to think and work in their own style. Allow them time and room to manoeuvre and be individuals. Let them take walks or work in non-traditional ways and spaces. Welcome a certain amount of chaos and accept that it's perfectly OK to do things in their own way. Encourage them to take risks. If they're great at their job and delivering results, it's far more valuable than if they work in a mandated orthodox method and sit at their desk from 9 to 5 because that is what the rules say. It will make managing people and projects a little more complicated, but it will make those same people and projects more productive, creative and positive. Because we all respond well to being trusted to deliver and having our skills validated.

A creative culture needs you to take as much of the corporate structure out of the way of the creative process as possible. All those ingrained, institutionalised, 'this is how we do it here' rules and behaviours must be open to challenge. It's easier said than done when you have client expectations and deadlines, but where there's a will ... All policy should be policy only until there is a better one, and anything that limits creativity, expression and exploration should be dismantled. There is no one right or wrong way. It will lead to a much healthier and more adaptable environment if you accept that everything is now just a work in progress.

Everybody comes to answers in their own way, and we've always encouraged that DIVERSITY OF ANSWERING QUESTIONS because when you start trying to impose systems or solutions on things, it's the opposite of creative chaos.

Nadja Lossgott
Joint CCO, AMV BBDO London

Lead by example. It's very difficult to create an environment where EVERYONE'S JUST TALKING about how you need to behave.

**Charlie Gatsky Sinclair
President Brands & Entertainment, Uncommon**

Psychological safety.

The importance of psychological safety at work became more widely appreciated thanks to Google's Project Aristotle. More than 100 teams were studied to discover the factors that led to effectiveness or high performance, and a clear component emerged: psychological safety. If team members do not feel safe to share their ideas, if they fear shame, humiliation or retaliation for an idea that fails, creativity dies. In a company environment where connection, trust and psychological safety have been forged, magic will happen. Building psychological safety into the everyday working practices of your agency will enable project teams to achieve great things. The bonds this forms will be instrumental in helping to create an environment that encourages creative thinking and experimentation.

You'll need to lead the way with your own behaviour, before encouraging it in others. Admitting when you're wrong or have messed up is a great way of saying it's OK to be wrong or mess up. We all do it. No one is perfect. It's nothing to be ashamed of, because failure is essential to success. Opening up about your own vulnerabilities will make it clear that you won't judge others for theirs. It also proves that you don't have to be an infallible superhero to progress in your career, and that will encourage everyone to keep trying.

Always be open to feedback. You're never too important to listen to how others view you or your thinking. This gives everyone a voice and the confidence to use it. Seeking out others' opinions and asking for their help shows that you value their input and don't expect them to struggle on their own to get something done.

Finally, conflict is inevitable in a business of passionate, creative people, but always seek to manage it without confrontation. Steer it away from the person and focus it on the reason.

The 'builds only' policy.

Much like improv, encourage everyone to run with a colleague's idea or thinking. Rather than going straight to the problems, which most people tend to do, just accept it and build on it. Immediately they'll feel the energy and the fun of freewheeling. It'll take them to new and interesting places – places that a 'no, not keen on that' won't. This breeds confidence, opens everyone's mind to different perspectives from their own, and fosters an environment where people aren't afraid to share original or progressive thoughts. Almost always, if there's nothing in it after all, it will peter out quickly and obviously, to be replaced enthusiastically by the next idea.

When you only talk about the problems or flaws in someone's thinking, you effectively shut down their idea and cut off communication. You also draw all the energy out of the room and leave that person feeling resentful or frustrated. People often do it to show seniority or to present themselves as more knowledgeable, but all it really says about them is that they are problem-spotters, and people soon learn not to share their early thinking with them. For a creative director, that is a bad place to be. You want everyone around the agency to feel that you are approachable and open to their thinking, and that you are supportive of everyone doing the same.

It's important during the creative iteration process that the critique is separated from the individual, and that it is constructive. The purpose of the critique should always be to progress the thinking that has been tabled, not to criticise the person or belittle their thinking. Invite everyone to introduce their ideas, listen to others' perspectives on the concept, improve on the idea, then produce a new iteration. After all, this is how most of the world's best and most innovative thinking is done.

I always think that when you start doing different-shaped work, you have to **WRAP IT IN OPTIMISM** and basically manifest it together. That's how it works. And for that, you have to trust everyone on your team, that you're all trying to pull together towards the best creative idea or the best creative execution.

Scott Dungate
CCO, Uncommon London

A diversity talent magnet.

We discussed the importance of cognitive diversity in Chapter 5. Encouraging diversity across the agency is no different. It doesn't have to be your agency's purpose, just your hiring policy. I would again encourage you to read *Rebel Ideas* by Matthew Syed to fully understand why, but, as the publisher's summary puts it: '*Rebel Ideas* offers a radical blueprint for creative problem-solving. It challenges hierarchies, encourages constructive dissent and forces us to think again about where the best ideas come from.'

Our brains are wired to make new connections from disparate inputs, but if those inputs aren't diverse, you can't expect to get fresh outputs; it will just be more of the same. It's pretty straightforward: a greater diversity of inputs makes for a greater diversity of creative outputs. The more different points of view you have, the better. Your creative culture, values and purpose will be the unifying forces. Although it's everyone's responsibility to make the agency culture a living, breathing thing, it's yours to enable it and to keep it on track. When a company commits itself to hiring diverse employees from different backgrounds and sexual orientations, it allows a glorious melting pot of ideas to bubble up. Diversity promotes a rich spectrum of perspectives, experiences, cultures, beliefs and reference points. Cultures like this are a magnet for fresh talent who don't always feel welcome or encouraged in more traditional creative businesses.

A creative culture doesn't happen by accident. It takes a lot of thought and effort, and the engagement of the entire business. It demands that you support and foster views that might not chime with yours. It asks everyone to be willing to share their ideas, and for those ideas to be received in a positive and open-minded environment that celebrates unique voices.

Don't work with idiots.

This should probably be the first point in this chapter, as every other point assumes that you are working with smart, open-minded people who come into work every day to do a good job. Dealing with idiots in your business who undermine your culture is easy enough once they are identified. It doesn't matter how good they are or, more commonly, how good they think they are, you just get rid of them as swiftly as possible, and make it clear to the rest of the business why. You are judged as a leader by the people you are willing to tolerate.

The harder ones to deal with are the idiots who are clients, or work for production companies or other agencies. This is part of every agency's ecosystem of dependencies. No agency can exist in a bubble. Unfortunately, you don't have any control over the culture of collaborators, and it's inevitable that you will come across people who don't place the same value on a strong creative culture as you do.

There will always be flashpoints and periods when your team are under pressure to deliver a project. But if a client or partner is consistently overstepping your boundaries, you need to deal with it. External forces can destroy your creative culture as easily as internal forces, with unrealistic demands or timings and negative, disrespectful attitudes. In the real world, you can't turn your back on every partner who doesn't sync with your culture. But you can make it clear to them that your creative culture is vital to the success of your agency, and therefore vital to their success, too. Then, if they still don't act appropriately, you have a business-critical decision to make.

Don't expect people to take seriously your claims that a creative culture matters to you if you aren't prepared to protect it. It's up to you to make it clear to external partners where your boundaries are. If you don't, you can't expect them to know.

Credit where credit is due.

This is probably the easiest way to support a creative culture. Hopefully you do it already, because you're just a decent person. But when a business is careful to assign credit for a project to deserving individuals and teams, the belief that the business is fair and makes an effort to recognise everyone for their contribution will encourage employees to give their best, because they know they are being seen and appreciated. Crediting the relevant team signals that you value team players, and everyone within that team equally, which will encourage the right cultural behaviours across the business. Remember, the way you behave determines the culture.

Make sure everyone in the team is credited, not just the key individuals. All projects are a team effort. No project in our industry ever sees the light of day without many hands helping, so call them all out. It matters. Include the placements, the clients, the PMs. Don't leave anyone's efforts uncelebrated, or that person will be the weak, disgruntled link in the chain next time. Within reason, credit can be shared without limit. Just look at the credits at the end of a movie. I don't know what a key grip does or how much their efforts affected my enjoyment of the film, but the key grip knows, and they want to be lauded for it because it shows that they played their part. Having your name associated with good work also builds careers.

Giving credit where credit's due will always reflect well on you. It demonstrates confident leadership, regardless of your title. It shows that you aren't seeking credit for yourself or wanting to shine brighter than anyone else in the team. That's never a good leadership look, and it won't endear you to anyone inside or outside the agency. Noisy attention-seeking creative leaders are not popular, unless they're being noisy on behalf of the team.

Check the credits and make sure that credit goes where it's due. IT'S YOUR RESPONSIBILITY to make sure that people get the credit for their work. If you have any power at all, it's in service of what you're trying to achieve together.

Lynsey Atkin
Former CCO, McCann London

Everyone's looking for a FUCKING PROCESS. But actually, it's a mindset.

Rob Campbell
CSO, Colenso NZ

Embrace gang culture.

My pet hate has always been people referring to their agency as being like a family. It's delusional. Your colleagues aren't family. Your family can't fire you. Your family love you unconditionally, even when you mess up. I could go on.

But agencies can be a great 'gang' to be a part of. Gangs are built on genuine connections. The best agency experiences I had felt like being part of a gang. Consider the traits of a gang that you could learn from:

Code Gangs have a shared set of values that all members buy into. The best live by their shared code, and discipline or exclude those who break it.

Aim Gangs have a mission and they make sure everyone, internally and externally, knows what it is. Most have a simple and achievable objective for the group.

Loyalty Great gangs are loyal to each other because they love and trust each other. They take time to decide who to admit and have a set of expectations for those they allow in. Not everyone gets in.

Pride Gang members love the gang and are proud to tell people they are part of it. They feel part of something special. People should be proud to say where they work.

Enemy All the best gangs, tribes and clubs have an enemy. Who is occupying your rightful turf? Whose failure would mean your success? Who don't you want to be like?

Iconic symbols Most gangs have a set of powerful symbols and messaging that allow them to identify themselves to each other and to others.

If you spend time and energy applying the above to your agency, you will create a powerful group of individuals who walk a little taller and speak with confidence to partners, clients or prospects. Because confidence is attractive, you'll 'win' more than you 'lose'.

Environment.

Anywhere that you spend a large part of your waking life, and where you're expected to perform to the peak of your abilities, must have an overwhelmingly positive impact on your well-being and productivity or it has failed in its purpose. A creative culture needs a creative environment to flourish in. I don't mean it has to be cool. Cool is transient and in the eye of the beholder. Far more important is that it understands and supports the needs of creativity and puts everyone at ease.

To encourage a greater diversity of talent, a creative environment has to make everyone feel welcome. It must provide facilities that cater to diverse needs and interests: a coffee area that sits at the heart of the space and encourages connections; comfortable collaboration spaces; disability access that isn't an afterthought; relaxation spaces; quiet spaces for working in peace; and so on. A thoughtfully designed workspace should help to reduce stress as well as enhance productivity. For instance, the use of natural building materials, natural furnishings and plants has an incredibly calming effect. I recently visited a well-known creative agency and they were experimenting with beautiful, natural fragrances in their reception. It brilliantly broke down the formality you expect from an office and made me feel at home immediately.

It's also enormously beneficial to have access to outdoor space. Realistically, few businesses in city-centre locations can afford that, but do try to make sure that there is plenty of natural light and that the windows have views. Ideally, they will even open to allow in fresh air and the street sounds from outside. Consider an eclectic mix of furniture, objects and art that spark conversation and inspiration. Incorporate diverse themes and diverse cultures and place them side by side. The more you try to curate this content, the less authentic it will feel, so allow everyone to influence it.

Creativity training.

So, you're a highly creative business that doesn't offer creativity training or do anything to promote creative activities outside work? Explain that one to me again? You want people to be creative, open-minded and curious across the entire business, but you're not investing in doing anything to promote that or help enable it, or even to show that you value those skills? Even if I told you that, according to research, businesses that invest in creativity training for their employees see a marked increase in the quality of their creative output very quickly? That would seem like a missed opportunity for a business looking to establish a creative culture, and a missed opportunity to bring down department barriers.

Encouraging and supporting all employees to pursue their creative interests fosters a culture that values individuality and celebrates diversity. Engaging in activities that involve experimentation and exploration cultivates a workplace mindset to match. Employees involved in creative endeavours outside work bring fresh perspectives into work, and when they are accustomed to taking creative risks in their personal pursuits, they apply the same mindset to their professional endeavours – especially if the business has taken an active role in supporting them. As a bonus, when employees engage in activities they are passionate about, their mental, emotional and even physical well-being improve.

So, not only will creativity training up people's creative game, it will also increase productivity, improve their mental health and reduce their sick days. It levels the creative playing field and allows everyone to demonstrate their creative capabilities. Making creativity talks, workshops and classes part of what the business offers everyone is a powerful, tangible signal that you're serious about building an inclusive creative culture.

9
The commercials of creativity.

The main reason creative directors rarely engage in the 'commercials' of advertising is that it doesn't remotely interest most of us. Simple as that, really. We weren't the kids at school who got gold stars for maths, economics or the sciences. We were the dreamers who got lost in the beauty of English literature, art and the humanities.

Numbers have never played a big part in our lives; they belong to a world that speaks in a language that means little to us, inhabited by people who are driven by very different motivations. They see the world in neat columns, made up of right and wrong answers, while we're more comfortable in chaos and glorious ambiguity. I've lost count of the finance meetings in which I glazed over, even when I was trying especially hard to concentrate. Spreadsheets, EBITs, amortisation and org charts are not what gets us out of bed in the morning. We're too distracted by the pursuit of brilliant ideas, emotive scores and great edits – which is, after all, what we're paid for and judged on.

You could decide that this chapter doesn't apply to you. That you're just too busy, the business employs lots of brilliant people to worry about the money, and it's best if everyone focuses on what they're good at. You'd have a reasonable point, and certainly plenty of company in that belief. But the reality is that advertising and communications is a business just like any other. It exists to make a profit, so that you can afford to pay people well and make decisions based on your values, not out of desperation. The sooner you accept that, the better your chances of building a strong and sustainable department and agency whose focus is on the good stuff, not in railing from one quarter to another.

That responsibility is with you now as a leader in the business, and you will be expected to take it seriously. Ignoring it will frustrate everyone around you and leave creativity unrepresented in key conversations that affect the way the business is run. The bottom line is that controlling the commercials gives a creative director far greater influence over their own destiny. And who doesn't want that?

There's no need to buy a briefcase and calculator, take evening classes in accountancy or give up lots of time you don't have to become a business titan. And you don't need to know everything from day one. Just be open to the topic. Engage when it is brought up. Don't roll your eyes and say, 'I'm creative, I don't do the numbers.' Don't be tempted to play to the dated stereotype of the creative director who doesn't sully their hands with the vulgarities of commerce and wave it all away dismissively. Take an active role and confound the mistrust that has built up between creatives and finance.

Ask lots of questions. Use the curiosity that has got you where you are to question how the whole thing works. Because that 'whole thing' is having the most enormous impact on your ability to get better work out the door. Put pressure on the people around you to explain to you the financial implications of your and their actions, and, most importantly, don't feel dumb for asking. Very soon you won't feel dumb or need to ask, and will start to look at the business with a far greater understanding of how it works. That will in turn make a positive difference to everyone who works for you.

I hope this chapter will convince you of the benefits of engaging with the business commercials. But if, by the end of it, you still want to have nothing to do with them, at least you'll have a better understanding of the control you are relinquishing.

There are three very simple rules that drive everything we do. We call them the trinity. **MAKE THE BEST WORK WE POSSIBLY CAN. HAVE FUN. MAKE A LIVING.** Always in that order. I can imagine that's a really hard thing to do, though, if every decision within your organisation is driven by the bottom line.

Katie Mackay-Sinclair
Partner, Mother London

My advice is to develop a relationship with the CFO. Have an open dialogue with them so that, rather than creating a demand every once in a while, you have an ongoing dialogue.
NO ONE LIKES SURPRISES, PARTICULARLY CFOs.

David Spencer
CFO, Goodby Silverstein & Partners SF

Make friends with finance.

To increase your chances of doing a brilliant job, you take time to build a relationship with your CEO, MD and business directors, you take time to build a relationship with your CSO, head of strategy and strategy directors, you take time to build a relationship with your CPO and senior producers. So why not the CFO or FD? Start your journey to understanding the commercials by taking the time to build a relationship with your CFO and senior members of their department. Go and introduce yourself. Take them out for coffee. Explain that you want to understand better how the business operates. They will be delighted to show you how it all works, and what the financial implications of each of your decisions are. They can give you a simple grounding in the basic financial model of the business and what the key levers are.

Right now, your brain may well atrophy when it's faced with Excel spreadsheets, but that's only because you don't yet understand how to read or interpret them. To date, your experience has probably involved being chased for answers about things you don't fully understand and unsurprisingly struggle to engage with. That will change when you get ahead of the ask. Before long, you'll realise just how simple it all is at its core, and feel a lot less intimidated. Running the finances of a creative business certainly isn't easy, but it's not complicated either.

None of us got into this industry to get more involved in the agency finances, and no creative on their way up has ever given finance a moment's thought (if they did, it was only as a department of people who spoiled everyone's fun). But it's part of your job now and the more you commit to getting your head around it, the less you'll be beholden to everyone else to make important agency and departmental decisions for you. The time has come. Go hug finance.

Resource percentages.

This isn't straightforward, as a lot depends on the type of agency, the overall headcount and, frankly, whom you ask. But as a guide, there is a staff cost split that enables the ideal functioning of an agency. A 'creative' agency, by which I mean an agency that puts a big emphasis on its creative product, will have a creative staff cost that is close to 40% of the total. It's fair to assume that it's a sliding scale from there: the lower the percentage, the lower the commitment to the creative product. Or, if the expectation for great creative is high but the percentage is low, you and the creative department will be expected to work extremely hard and relentlessly over-deliver, which will condense your time on briefs, your time in production and your ability to think things through properly, inevitably leading to fatigue, burnout and a sweatshop reputation. It's definitely worth asking about staff cost split in an interview if you want to really understand the creative ambition of an agency.

In *Confessions of an Advertising Man* (1963), David Ogilvy observed: 'In most agencies, account executives outnumber the copywriters two to one. If you were a dairy farmer, would you employ twice as many milkers as you had cows?' It's down to you to change this if you're under-resourced. Talk it through with your leadership team. They will of course defend the need for their disciplines, as the current percentages will represent the status quo. You'll hear that the clients won't accept fewer account people on their accounts, and that planning doesn't have enough people as it is, and production and project management have been stripped to the bone, etc. But the reality is that there is absolutely no reason for a client to come to an agency if they aren't getting the best possible work. All the best account management, planning and creative cultures in the world count for nothing if the work is ordinary because there aren't enough people to do it properly.

Wieden's is almost **TWO CREATIVE PEOPLE TO ONE ACCOUNT PERSON.** We aim for two to one.

Bronwen Hemming
FD, Wieden + Kennedy London

Project scopes are put together by the account people. What tends to happen is that the account person will try to create a structure to hit the number the client has given them. Let's say the client's got £1 million and the account person puts together a structure that gets to £1.3 million. The only way to bring the number down is to shave the amount of time you get. So, the account person goes, 'WHERE CAN I SHAVE A WHOLE LOT OF TIME OFF? CREATIVE RESOURCE!' Because they don't look at it anyway. In a very unconsciously biased way, they are protecting themselves. If the account people have put together a team structure for X, I think it's legitimate to ask how much of the overall fee is to do with creative.

David Spencer
CFO, Goodby Silverstein & Partners SF

Resource scoping.

What? Resource scoping?!? (Also known as account or project scoping.) I didn't know anything about it either until I was on my second CCO job. Involvement should start at creative director level, but no one ever thinks to include them in this, probably because historically, creative directors just weren't interested. It's also possible that account management aren't that keen to involve you, because they have gone light on the creative time and resource allocation. That's why it's not uncommon to find that there isn't enough creative time or resource for a project. I'm not suggesting that it's a premeditated act to nobble you – it's more their understanding of what it might take to do a good job, rather than yours – but it will nobble you, nevertheless.

In simple terms, you need to be clear on exactly how much your business will earn from an account or project. You then subtract from that the cost of the fixed overheads you need to cover and the profit you want to make. What's left is the amount you have to resource that account or project. This will always be a point of contention. You'll want as much resource and time as possible to do the best work you can, because that's what you're judged on, and finance and account management will want to make as much money as possible. What makes it hard is that both sides are correct in their demands, so you'll have to find a compromise. But if you aren't involved in the conversation, there's only ever going to be one outcome.

Why would you not insist that a scope needs your agreement on resource allocation and timings before it can go to a client? You don't need to write the scope, or get particularly deep into it; leave that to account management, project management and finance. But do ask that you are taken through it. It won't take long, and whatever time it does take will be time you'll save pushing for more time and resource to get the project completed.

Project creep.

When it comes to the profitability of a project, every decision you make as creative director has a financial consequence. Every extra team you put on a brief, every extra week you take, will make the project less profitable. (Although the unpredictability of creative development will always make it hard to determine exactly what it will take, so any agency worth its salt will build in a contingency to allow for that.)

Understand the financial implications of a brief upfront, before anyone does anything. Then allocate time and resource accordingly, depending on what you want to achieve from the brief. We all know that all projects are not equal, that a reasonable percentage of the work that goes through your department doesn't need you to go all guns blazing on it; it just needs pragmatic handling. Be clear with yourself which are the opportunities that you need to invest in. I always wanted everything to be a 10 and found it hard to let some projects be less than that, but you have to pick your battles or you simply won't have the cushion to go all out when you need to.

A good creative agency will always be ready to invest in the overburn if the potential for a piece of work is good enough. Great work changes everything, because it creates fame for the client *and* the agency, which attracts new business and talent, and boosts morale. All that will always massively outweigh the investment of making it as good as it can be.

For the remainder, make sure you don't waste money that you could be reinvesting in people, training and projects that need it. In an ideal world you wouldn't need to consider this. You would make enough profit to cover it. But you don't. No one does. As agency fees continue to be challenged and timings become ever tighter, you're going to have to get smarter about what you prioritise.

I would expect my creative partners to have a level of understanding that if we throw loads of resource at something, that impacts our profitability. **THAT DOESN'T MEAN WE SHOULDN'T DO THAT FOR THE RIGHT OPPORTUNITY**, but it requires a conversation and an understanding of that investment. It's not that hard to understand the basics of how you make money.

Helen Andrews
CEO, Johannes Leonardo NY

Some of the best creative leaders have had a business head on them. DAVID DROGA. NILS LEONARD. JOHN HEGARTY. If you want to work at a creatively driven agency, the driving isn't just in the creative work. It has to be in the business as well.

Scott Dungate
CCO, Uncommon London

Cash is king.

You will always need the ability to pay your bills. And you need cash to do that. If you can't meet your bills, you will go under. Many people argue that cash is the most important way to judge a company. There's an expression that finance often use: Turnover is vanity, profit is sanity, but cash is king.

You don't really need to get into the nitty-gritty of this, but you do need to know that whatever you or anyone else in your department spends comes from the cash that the business is holding in reserve to pay the bills. Every business-class flight rather than economy, every taxi instead of public transport, every big lunch. It never seems like much, but multiply it by all the people in the business and every working day and it soon mounts up. Consider ways to be resourceful and encourage your teams to do the same. Make everyone justify their expenses. Margins and profits are under immense pressure these days, and making money in adland has never been harder.
Your business really doesn't need a hole in the bucket.

This cash reserve is the same cash reserve that provides the funds to invest in awards, events and training. The same cash reserve that means you can fund that exciting project that needs the agency to invest in it for it to reach its creative potential. The same cash reserve that will enable you to award bonuses in recognition of team members who go above and beyond. Basically, it's the cash reserve that funds all the things that make work more interesting, rewarding and exciting. The bigger the cash reserve, the better for everyone.

It really comes down to how you want to spend the company's money. Do you fritter it away on a few upgrades and lunches, or do you enlist it to help you to make the work and the workplace better? This is definitely a conversation that you should be having with your department. It will be news to them.

Time sheets.

Time sheets have been a battleground since time began. The mere mention of time sheets is enough to make every creative person who has ever been chased for one roll their eyes and groan. Everyone hates time sheets, except people in finance. And no, it's not because they enjoy making your life harder. Finance people like time sheets because they provide data that informs the vital decisions that drive the profitability of the business. And that is something you should be a big supporter of, because at the heart of every successful business – even the world's most creative businesses – lies a focus on productivity and profitability.

Full disclosure: I was once a time-sheet hater. I avoided contact with them at all costs, fearing that they might somehow be used to steal my creative soul. But then a very smart person in finance explained them to me. Time sheets track the time spent on projects to allow accurate billing. They're also used to inform accurate project proposals based on time sheets for previous projects. Accurate time tracking isn't there to spy on you or the creative department for some nefarious end; it's simply there to ensure that the business is compensated fairly for the work done. Basically, time sheets are on your side.

Time sheets mean you can make sure the right level of resource is attached to a project and that the client can be held to account if they become too demanding. They protect your department from being exploited.

But time sheets work only if they are filled in and don't have to be chased for weeks on end. Perhaps it's time you explained why they matter to your department, or asked someone in finance to do it. Think of it as an opportunity to educate your teams about this being a business that needs to be profitable to enable them to have a job.

Department budgets.

I was trusted to solve complex business problems and set the creative vision for some of the world's biggest and most influential brands, but I wasn't trusted to control my own departmental budget. I found it frustrating that every time I wanted to hire someone, fire someone or give someone a raise or bonus, I had to ask the grown-ups for money. This does nothing to reassure the creative department or the agency more widely that you are a key decision-maker in the business. It undermines you. But it's the industry norm.

What's really frustrating, though, is that this was a situation almost entirely of my own making, and I didn't realise it. I only ever considered my own department's needs and made demands without thinking about the rest of the agency. To be able to look after your department means having to understand the entire agency's wage needs, how the creative department fits into that, and how the needs of the agency can ebb and flow. It's also about considering the structure of your department based on how you prefer to work. Are there too many seniors, not enough seniors, not enough hungry young teams, and so on? Are the teams you have good value for what they produce? Are you able to use them effectively on your accounts? Is there a healthy diversity? Is there enough income to justify them all? It's not complicated, but the new normal means that it is in constant flux, which has definitely made it harder.

If you want to understand your department budget better, so that you can make considered decisions and not just siloed demands, speak to your CFO and CEO. Ask for their help and advice and work with them as a team. Planning ahead and setting long-term budgets is close to impossible as projects become more commonplace and clients are reluctant to agree to longer than thirty-day notice periods. But together you stand a much better chance of getting there.

With the very best agencies, the headlines are about them winning new business. But actually, **THEIR COMMERCIAL SECRET** is that they don't lose any business.

Charlie Rudd
CEO, Creative Practice, Publicis Groupe UK

Pitches and new business.

As I mentioned in Chapter 7, the average cost of a pitch in the UK is £50,000, and the average pitch success rate is 1 in 3. So, on average, it costs an agency £150,000 to win one new piece of business. For clarity, though, that's not £150,000 that is sitting around and could have given fifty people a £3,000 bonus each, or paid for a £75,000 senior creative team to ease the pressure on the department. It's not a pot of money you could have spent elsewhere. It's people hours and agency running costs, money that is already accounted for in the fixed costs of the business.

If those fixed costs aren't being covered by clients, they will have to be reduced by improving your win ratio, putting more time and resource into expanding your existing client relationships, or making people redundant. The best new business wins come from existing business. Often, they aren't big PR-worthy news and don't feel that exciting to win, but they beat pitching, partly because of the costs we've already mentioned but also because they show that you're getting in deeper with a client and securing the relationship in the long term. Long-term clients are great clients for all sorts of reasons, both financial and creative. Don't save all your most glittering efforts for new clients.

You have to go into every pitch believing that you are going to win it. Of course you do. But if you're tilting at windmills you might want to reconsider. You also need a criterion for pitching, rather than just saying yes to every pitch you're offered. We've all done it, and all regretted it. Put your focus into fewer and go harder. If the pitch doesn't offer you the opportunity to make famous work that would drive more new business, to make enough money to be profitable, or to expand your business or creative offer in an interesting way, question why you're doing it.

Production budgets.

First, if you know what the production budget is, don't write or present something that can't possibly be done for that amount. It's not someone else's problem – it's yours. Ignoring budget constraints destroys the client's trust in you, and makes you look as though you don't know what you're doing. In collaboration with a producer or project manager before you present a proposal, work out what's possible to make it happen, and if it's too much of a stretch, rewrite it or start again. Every client will appreciate you trying to find innovative ways to stretch their budget, but it's a rare client who is OK with being presented work they can't afford, particularly if it happens regularly. If you show work to a client, they have every right to expect that you can make it for them. Every climb-down from then on dents their trust in you, their respect for your abilities and ultimately their desire to stay at the agency.

Second, don't let the creative department go to town on a campaign brief when you don't know the approximate production budget. We've all done it – presented the most extraordinary creative tour de force that includes the documentary pilot, the cinema and TV roadblocks, extravagant experiential, celebrity socials, special-build tech-first OOH, elaborate apps, product and a host of other things that you thought were cool. The clients are thrilled with your wonderful work and ambition on their behalf, and with being made to feel amazing. But this isn't a fine-art project, it's a business, and the more of our time and work clients pay for, the better the business will do. Unless there's the money to make it all, it's a colossal waste of time at your expense. And, as fun as it is to write it, it's demotivating when it all goes in the bin and the only thing you make are some idents and pre-rolls. You might also find that the creative department don't find your 'big opportunity' speech quite so rousing next time.

Talent acquisition.

Chances are that by the time you're in a position to hire creatives, you will already have a relationship with a couple of headhunters, especially if they have helped you with moves yourself. They aren't silly. Putting people into top jobs is their new business strategy, and you trust them because they have supported you, so of course you'll use them when you look to build your new department. Tell them about your plans. Keep them updated. That way, not only will they keep looking out for you personally because they know you'll bring them business with every department rebuild, but also they will let you know of great talent that might be up for a move before it goes public. It can be a valuable, symbiotic relationship.

The only downside is cost. Many agencies now shy away from using headhunters for anything other than the most prestigious roles because of the costs involved. Most headhunters charge about 20% of the first year's salary of any candidate they find for you, and that is obviously double for a team. Even if you negotiate it down, it's still a big chunk out of your budget, which is why the big networks have invested in their own talent search teams.

If that's the case with your agency, get to know the team. Brief them on your plans and keep them close. They don't come out of your budget, so they are a free resource as far as you're concerned. They will also be incredibly motivated to find you the right person. You will have to work harder with an in-agency team than with headhunters, since they won't be at the centre of the industry's constant job fluctuations and won't have the same inside knowledge or extensive connections. You will need to write your own target lists, so it's essential that you and your other senior creatives stay up to date with who is doing good work and where they are.

10
Adapting to change.

As the adage correctly has it, the only constant is change. And few things date quicker than a creative director who isn't willing to keep up. During the course of your creative directing career, you will face many new and unfamiliar challenges that you'll be expected to have a point of view on, since they may in some way impact your role, the creative department, the agency more broadly or even the direction of the industry.

I've been through the digital revolution, going from magic-marker layouts to laptops, integration, media fragmentation, from film to files, the rise of virals, social media, the smartphone, apps and influencers, SEO, the development of content, AR, VR, the metaverse, and so on. In fact, I can't even remember all the big new things that have changed the course of my working life. Some were short-lived and over-hyped, and others became truly transformational. I was expected to have a point of view on all of them, because you never know at first which are which, despite what everyone claims after the event. It pays to go into them all with an open mind.

The biggest challenge today is how to embrace the possibilities of AI. But I want to focus on how to approach change, whatever it is. Because the one thing you can be certain of is that there will be something after AI that changes everything all over again. And, as change continues to speed up, it's unlikely to be far away.

You'll never have all the answers and be the keeper of all the knowledge. Don't put that pressure on yourself. But you do need to find out what the new thing means, and what positive and negative impacts are likely to result from it. Then you have to decide how best to commit time, resources and budget to it.

Being able to determine how your business decides to adapt to the next challenge is both an exciting position to be in and a big responsibility. In almost all industries, change is not just important, it's essential. Customer needs are constantly evolving, and they expect you to evolve to meet them. If you want to stay competitive and relevant, you need to view your approach as a constant work in progress. This means always being open to new ideas, taking calculated risks and experimenting. Recognise that change is inevitable and be prepared to adapt as circumstances evolve.

There is another enormous benefit to being open to change that will affect you more personally. The more you do it, the more you want to do it. Humans aren't good at uncertainty, and change makes everyone feel uncomfortable. But those of us who can push through those feelings come out at the other side with the confidence of knowing they have the adaptability and resilience to do it successfully, and the skills to adapt more easily to whatever comes next. This diminishes the fear of change. Sticking to what you know and not being open to moving forward spell death for a creative director. Dated views, dated skill sets and dated references are not tolerated for long by agencies or clients. Change gives you a reason to keep learning and challenging yourself.

When you demonstrate willingness and enthusiasm to remain relevant, it gives everyone around you the confidence to follow your lead and creates a more future-facing environment. It also makes you a 'go-to' person the next time something new and interesting pops up.

Aim to be as informed as possible. Seek wise counsel and get beyond the hype and the headlines. Experience it for yourself. Experiment. Play with it. Just don't turn your back on it until you're sure it's not going to be a benefit to the business. And even then, be prepared that you won't always get it right.

As a creative director today, you have to **UNLEARN EVERYTHING YOU LEARNED YESTERDAY.** In our careers, we've gone through the most profound change in communication, and in how people receive information, since time began.

Richard Brim
Former CCO, Adam & Eve DDB London

Optimism, not cynicism.

Cynicism is for creative wet blankets. It's easy and lazy to be cynical, and generally that's where people who feel threatened go to hide. Be open-minded and investigate before you draw any conclusions. The cynics said digital images would never replace film. Well, guess what? The cynics also said streaming would never replace owning music. Well, guess what?

This doesn't mean you have to rush at every 'next big thing' with your arms wide open and declare undying love for it. Just don't be a grouch about it because you think it all seems a bit far-fetched. Just because you can't see it happening doesn't mean it won't. One of the clearest examples of cynics getting it wrong is an article in *Wired* magazine in February 1995 talking about the imminent demise of the internet: 'Most things that succeed don't require retraining 250 million people.' You don't get much more wrong than that.

Cynics believe themselves to be the informed voice of reason in a world gone mad. But mostly their views are uninformed and unimaginative. It's understandable in some ways why people default to being cynical; after all, it's human nature to frame the future with what you understand from the present. And if it seems like too big a behavioural shift, it gets discounted. But that's flawed logic, and incredibly uncreative, because truly innovative advances always come from left field. They don't come about in neat, tidy, easy-to-understand packages, the product of clear, critical thinking; they arrive out of nowhere in messy, odd, amorphous packages, the outpouring of original creative thinking. They need nurturing and iteration. So don't reject them because they aren't immediately clear or fully formed.

Being the person who rejects the new and the next will date you very quickly. It might also suggest that you aren't the progressive creative hotshot the agency wants as its figurehead. Optimism is a great habit to get into.

You've got to leave cynicism at the door and SHOW UP NAKED. Try to start every day that way.

Rodrigo Sobral
Global CCO, Oliver

When you get to a senior position, you have to embrace change and **KEEP THE LEARNING CURVE STEEP.** If you just try to hold on to that yesteryear model, you're finished.

Bill Scott
CEO, Droga5 London

Knowledge is power.

Imagine if doctors stopped learning about advances in medical science when they left medical school. If they stopped researching, training, reading up on the latest thinking, going to seminars and conferences. We'd still be bloodletting to get rid of a headache. How we approach creative direction will always be influenced by the tools, tech and trends available to us. As change accelerates, awareness of those options matters more than ever.

The idea will always come first, but the format in which it can be presented to a consumer will forever change. The more you and everyone around you know, the less you'll get caught out or passed by. Encourage conversation focused on what's new and interesting, not just in the creative department but around the entire agency. Who knows where the biggest changes or most interesting new formats will come from? This also sends a strong message to the department that you support an open creative culture. Inspiration could come from articles, books, podcasts, talks, events or coaching. But choose your sources carefully. As much as everyone loves a good case study, tread with caution since, as you well know, they are only ever a plumped and preened version of the truth, and there will be lots of people out there keen to show how ahead of the curve they are by putting one out.

Encourage learning with a programme of talks and workshops on new and exciting discoveries in tech and media. Send someone off to learn new skills so that they can pass them on to everyone else. Foster curiosity. Share interesting articles on surprising topics. Consider making it a cross-departmental team's responsibility to find and share new thinking to get some momentum behind it. The more you are seen to promote progressive new ideas and formats, the better. You determine the culture, and people will follow your lead.

Be clear on why.

OK, so you're open-minded and informed about all the latest opportunities that could enhance your ability to build the business, to make it more relevant and creatively stronger than ever. Suddenly, you spot the big opportunity. You're pumped and want to make it happen. Optimistic for what it will help you and your agency to achieve. Great! Exciting times. But before you rush off in pursuit of it, pause for a moment.

Is there a clear need for this change, or is it just a nice-to-have? Interrogate it with your leadership team. Will it improve what you currently offer? Will it give you a credible opportunity for new business? Is it a good fit culturally? Is it financially viable for you to implement it properly? Do you have the resource bandwidth to commit to seeing it through? Who will lead the project? Should you partner with someone who already has the capability, or should you build your own capability? Assess the skills you already have and who it would be good to involve alongside you. Consider the outcome you want and what is a realistic time frame for achieving it, then build a roadmap to get you there and get everyone in leadership to sign up to it. The biggest cause of change programmes failing in business is a lack of senior management alignment. Building a clear case for why you should do it not only de-risks the changes you want to make, but also gives you the answers to the questions that everyone will inevitably ask. You are more likely to take colleagues on the journey with you if you can help them to understand exactly why you're doing it.

No matter how convinced you are that this is the big one, don't bet your house on it. You don't need to completely overhaul your business all at once – you'll send it into shock. Start with small changes, introducing them to your business in unthreatening, easy-to-understand chunks.

Focus on the positives.

I've been careful to keep my personal feelings out of most of this book. But there is one topic that I'm compelled to vent on: the obsessive moaning about how advertising was better in the old days. This thumb-sucking, comfort-blanket narrative is perpetuated by a noisy few to keep a spotlight on their former glories. Glories that were forged in a different industry era, when time, money and experience were all in abundance. It's healthy to celebrate the industry's legacy – a lot can be learned by studying what has gone before – but it serves no purpose to constantly lament its passing or wistfully ache for its return. The future never looks like the past. Get over it. Advertising hasn't gone to hell in a handcart, it has simply changed with the shifting sands of societal and economic need. If advertising isn't relevant to its time, it serves no purpose.

Lamenting the past does nothing to excite the next generation about the potential for the industry's future, either. And your job is to do just that. So be positive about change – if you can't, there will be someone who can. Everyone needs to believe that you believe that the changes you want to implement will result in a better outcome, that the business will be better able to stay strong and relevant, and that all the anxiety and upheaval of change will be worth it in the long run.

It's also worth reminding yourself that these are good problems to have. The need for managing change wouldn't exist if your business wasn't staying relevant or planning for growth. A business in the advertising industry that is clinging to a past set of circumstances won't be around for long. An increase in your likelihood of survival and success is the biggest positive outcome of change, and a good thing to focus on. If need be, it's a good thing to remind everyone else to focus on, too.

Overcoming the fear.

Change brings with it a great deal of fear. 25% of Brits claim to be too scared to try anything new; 50% claim to hate change of any sort; and 71% say they find change hard to cope with.* More than 9 million Brits have eaten the same breakfast every day for at least the last five years. The human brain has a frustrating habit of defaulting to known behaviour at the first opportunity because we find it reassuring. So don't expect everyone to jump up and down with excitement at the prospect of your brilliant new plan, no matter how truly brilliant it might be. You have to be realistic about how hard it is to bring about change in an organisation that has probably functioned quite happily the same way for some time. Resistance to change is a common reason for the failure of change initiatives.

Fear is contagious. How you respond publicly to change and how positively you communicate it make a huge difference to it landing successfully. Remaining calm in the face of change will get you a lot further than running around in a panic. Have the debates with your team behind closed doors, get aligned, then communicate what has to be said in a positive manner. You need to be the embodiment of confidence.

Fear must also be managed in an empathetic manner. Take the time to listen to people's concerns. Acknowledge their fears; don't dismiss them or become irritated if people don't immediately accept your vision. You'll only create a vacuum that will be filled with misunderstanding and half-truths and make people worry more. Discuss them publicly if necessary. Make it clear that it's OK to admit to being worried. Getting people to open up about their anxiety will give you a better understanding of what you need to overcome to help everyone move forward. Listen and get feedback. If they feel safe, they will stay focused on their roles and deliver the change you need.

*www.freeagent.com/company/press-room/fear-of-change-research

There should be a sense of possibility, that **PEOPLE HAVE THE POWER TO CHANGE** things. You want them to follow you with their brains and not fear.

Charlie Gatsky Sinclair
President Brands & Entertainment, Uncommon

You don't have to be a practitioner. You have to be the person who says, 'All right, guys, I'm going to put a team together to really understand this and then play it back to us. Then we can take what they've learned and maybe SPRINKLE IT IN A FEW ACCOUNTS so we can all scale up.'

Bill Scott
CEO, Droga5 London

The task force.

As much as you might want to, you don't have time to get to the bottom of every new advance or trend. And it isn't the best use of your time to do that. But, as we've established, it's important that you don't ignore them. So spread the load. Select a small group of people to dig deep into a specific area that you think the business will benefit from, and present their findings. People are generally delighted to be asked to be part of a special ops team, especially if it's to investigate something interesting and innovative. Try to pick people who have a followership within the business, to make everyone more receptive to the topic.

Mix up the disciplines if you have the resources to do so. Not only will this give you a range of perspectives, but also, regardless of the outcome, it's a great way to encourage advocacy for something new across the agency, rather than siloing it into one department. You can then use the same people to apply their learnings to one of your more progressive accounts, to give you practical experience of the subject. No client will ever mind you being forward-thinking on their behalf. At this point you could look to widen the team and bring more people into the project to socialise the learnings.

Hopefully, it will all go to plan, and you'll end up with a first-hand case study to talk to other clients about, which offers great potential for new business. It's always worth remembering that many clients are under the same pressure as you to understand new technology or thinking that offers them a business advantage, and they will appreciate you sharing your learning, especially if it makes them look good to their organisation. It will also remind your clients what a smart and forward-thinking partner they have in you, and that they don't need to shop around for help with the latest trends.

The expert.

If there isn't time or resource to put together a task force to develop the learnings you need, it makes sense to look at bringing in someone who can be a beacon on the subject. This person can bridge the knowledge gap and accelerate change. They may not last in the long term as others catch them up, their knowledge is assimilated into the body of the agency and you all start to realise that it wasn't so complicated after all, or they could become an integral part of the team; either way, they will create momentum.

As with anything new, there won't be many deeply experienced experts to hand, and certainly very few who also understand how it applies to advertising. There will be no shortage of people claiming to be experts, however, who have spotted the opportunity for a quick career pivot, so move carefully. Make sure they are good communicators and keen to share their knowledge. Over the years, I've experienced a few experts who struggle to share their knowledge, deliberately keep it to themselves, or set out to baffle everyone with complexity, so that they retain a position of power. You don't want these people. They will do more harm than good, and put people off the one thing they are there to encourage.

It's your responsibility to be clear in the interview process exactly how your business works and where you see the new person helping. Bringing them in and not creating the conditions for them to engage with the business in the right way sets them up to fail. If they don't have an ad background, don't expect them to just slot in. This will be a costly failure, not just financially, and it will do nothing to encourage interest or belief in the change you want to implement. They will become disillusioned and leave, and that is not good for morale or for everyone's belief in management's ability to keep the agency moving forward.

It takes time.

The key to successful change in any business is to upset people only at a rate they can tolerate. That might sound harsh, but the reality is that people will always resist change, which makes changing behaviour notoriously difficult in any business, even a business in the creative industries. Allow time if you want to take the business with you. Don't expect to land a successful change programme overnight. Rushing into change is counterproductive, no matter how urgent the need.

Changing the way things work in your business will take up a lot of your time, often keeping you away from your day-to-day creative department responsibilities, which are demanding enough. You'll end up feeling as though you're not doing anything properly – and you probably won't be. To avoid burning out, allow yourself a realistic amount of time to be able to deliver on both. Don't let your enthusiasm or any external pressure get the better of your common sense.

Pushing for change too quickly can lead to burnout and increased resistance, but not demonstrating sufficient momentum can be equally damaging. It's a tough balance. Your teams will lose interest if the changes require behavioural shifts and sacrifice and are felt to be dragging on. So engineer a few early wins in the process. Build them into your plan from the beginning. As well as the big vision goals, put in a few more easily achievable goals, then celebrate and publicise them when they are reached. This positive reinforcement will help everyone feel as though they're winning and that change is not only achievable, but exciting. By harnessing the enthusiasm the short-term wins generate, you'll be in a better position to sustain the momentum for the long haul.

Upskilling.

The advertising and communications industry is historically not great at committing to upskilling its employees. Yet, as workplace tech innovations move at a furious pace and AI sweeps through numerous roles, there has never been a greater imperative to invest in it. Upskilling is the process of enhancing an employee's skills to meet the demands of evolving job roles, and it can take many forms, including online courses, formal qualifications, workplace training, mentoring and peer training.

Upskilling is important for employees and employers equally because it helps you both to stay relevant. It can also save you a great deal of time and money on recruitment, since finding people who are a cultural fit and have the new skills you want is a lot harder than training the people you already have to acquire those skills. If you don't commit to keeping your team up to date, expect them to go somewhere that will. They can't afford to fall behind on in-demand skill sets any more than you can. So, place a premium on people who already work for you and who are keen to develop their skills, because their willingness to adapt will help the business to meet new challenges in the future. And it's good to know who you'll be able to rely on.

There are many other benefits to upskilling. It is proven to enhance job satisfaction, which in turn increases retention rates. Who doesn't want to feel valued at work? By offering someone the chance to upskill, you are saying, 'I believe in you and want you to be part of this company's future.' This in turn increases productivity. A motivated, secure person with the right skills who believes in your culture is like gold dust.

In 2025 Gen Z will account for 20% of the workforce, and it's worth noting that members of this generation prioritise learning and career development. So upskilling is no longer an option, it's a necessity if you want to recruit the next generation.

The death of advertising.

I wish I had collected all the articles that proclaimed the death of advertising from the start of my career until now. I'd have enough for an entire book. They would be a hilarious cavalcade of posturing nonsense that we could all have a good chuckle over.

On average, at least a couple of senior members of the industry every year declare that advertising is dead. There are two types of person who write articles with this headline. One will be a well-known industry figure who has enjoyed considerable success in doing things a certain way, and now sees the landscape changing in a way they don't much like the look of, mostly because it affects their business or their legacy. Consequently, they assume that we're all doomed and that the bottom will fall out of the industry imminently. The other is someone who comes from a business with a challenger culture or represents a new business with a vested interest in whatever latest development everyone is frothed up about. They think this is now the only way forward, that everything that came before them is dusty and dated, and that we all need to drop what we're doing and follow them.

Every year they are both wrong. Advertising will never die. The need to advertise brands will remain as long as we have a free market economy. It's just in constant flux, and will continue to be for as long as it does exist, because it will continue to use whatever tools are available to find a competitive advantage. It has changed beyond recognition from the industry I joined as a junior copywriter. And it will keep changing, sometimes for the better, sometimes for the worse, depending on your point of view. So, whenever you read one of those articles, take it as a sign of an industry shift that you need to be aware of if you aren't already. Just don't take any notice of click-bait headlines.

11

The pros and cons of awards.

'Awards are the happy coincidence of doing the best work in the world.' Your level of interest in this chapter rather depends on whether or not you agree with that statement. I'm not going to waste my time writing, or your time reading, about how to win awards for the sake of winning awards, or how to game them. If that's your focus, skip the next sixteen pages; you won't find them very helpful.

Few topics in advertising are as certain to get everyone worked up as awards. Most people have a deeply entrenched view one way or the other. Awards are either the best or the worst thing ever, depending on whom you ask. I think they have the potential to be both those things. At their best they hold us all to account, keep creative standards high, motivate creative careers, help to educate the industry and reward the amazing efforts of all concerned. At their worst they are self-indulgent, scam-ridden, network-dominated and damaging to the integrity of the industry. There is no question that awards schemes are occasionally gamed and abused, and that the industry turns a blind eye to it. But it is in everyone's best interests that they are used appropriately to celebrate successful work, work that upholds the ambitions of those in the industry to be taken seriously as valuable partners to our clients.

This chapter focuses on how to take a healthy and productive approach to awards. I'm going to look at how they can be used to reward and encourage, and to build reputations, new business pipelines and pride in your business. My intention is simply to present the pros and cons with as much balance as possible. If you approach awards in a considered and informed way, you should be able to enjoy their many benefits while avoiding their pitfalls.

It would be disingenuous of me to say that awards didn't interest me or haven't played a big part in enabling the fulfilment of my career ambitions. They have been pivotal. They have enabled a life I could not have imagined when I started out. They gave me job opportunities and credibility; they de-risked me as a potential creative-director hire; and the more I won, the further they propelled me through the ranks.

To be honest, I have never chased awards. I've always set out to do famous work. Work that got talked about. I didn't game the system (maybe I would have won more if I had). But winning when you know you've cheated seems a hollow achievement to me. I only ever respected the agencies who set out to do the work that was right for the client, the business need and the brief, and, in doing so, to pursue something fresh, different and popular. From experience, I perfectly understand the pressure you can find yourself under to win awards at any cost and be tempted to game them. Network pressure, job security pressure, peer pressure and so on. It doesn't excuse it, but it does explain it. For as long as creatives and agencies stand to gain so much by winning awards, this pressure will continue, meaning that – for the time being, at least – the status quo will remain unaltered.

People sometimes think that great work happens by accident, that there is a huge amount of luck involved in the stars aligning, but fundamentally, it's smart people making **CONSIDERED DECISIONS** that are informed through years of taste and references.

Lynsey Atkin
Former CCO, McCann London

What is the single most important thing about advertising? It's awareness. Awards are a big part of driving awareness of your work, whether we like it or not. It's the same with creative people, creative reputation, creative agencies, whatever. IF PEOPLE DON'T KNOW WHO YOU ARE, YOU DON'T EXIST. Your job is to sell things. One of them has to be your agency.

Kevin Chesters
CSO, KC Consulting

Why bother?

The two main reasons for entering awards are to attract talent and new business. Creatives need to win awards to get pay rises, promotions, better briefs, respect, credibility and career longevity, and to attract headhunters, so they want to work where they have the best chance of winning them. Agencies need to win awards to make those award-winning creatives want to work for them. If an agency doesn't enter them, or ever win them, it won't attract or retain the best creative talent. Realistically, awarded creative work raises an agency's profile and establishes its reputation as a creative hot shop far more quickly than unawarded creative work.

Without a doubt, if your agency does great, award-winning work, attracting new business and pitching will be a lot easier too. Almost all clients who approach the top creative agencies to pitch have already decided that they want to work with them before the pitch begins. No CMO was ever fired for hiring the most creative agency in town. Awards and case studies are an accepted metric for success that de-risk the decision-making process and can be used to justify the decision to the boss. Ambitious clients also know that award-winning work will enhance their own reputation. Everyone benefits from having their name attached to awarded work.

It's important to note that clients will also be looking to make sure your fantastic award-winning work was extremely effective against the client's business metrics. And this is where scam work falls down. It wasn't created against a genuine client need, it didn't have full media support, and it almost certainly did next to nothing to benefit the client's business, so it lacks the robustness of real results. In most cases, too, top creatives don't want a reputation for winning with scammy ads, so they tend to avoid going to the agencies that have a reputation for scamming, regardless of how many 'Grand Prix' they have.

Time and cost.

There's no getting round this one. Awards are a big financial commitment, but approached in the right way they are also a great investment in your business. Start by engaging your leadership team in order to agree a budget, and where it will come from. The average cost of an entry at a major international awards show is £1,500, and it's a sliding scale down from there depending on the credibility and reach of the show. But it mounts up quickly. For example, if you decide to enter three big shows with one campaign that stretches over three or four categories in each show, you're already at about £20,000 just for entry fees.

Then you need to consider the cost of putting all the assets together. If they aren't beautifully executed, they won't get a look-in, because the competition is fierce and well funded, and won't be cutting corners. A well-executed case study is seriously expensive and time-consuming. If you can get all this done in-house, the cost is agency time and resource, but if not, you could end up easily doubling your entry fees in post-production costs. In mitigation, case studies are never wasted and have a wide range of uses outside the awards. Getting them done to an awards entry deadline can often stop them falling off your to-do list.

Another cost is the non-billable time you and the creatives will have to spend deciding what work is worthy of being entered and which awards shows to enter it in, agreeing on the categories, checking eligibility, writing the submissions and pulling together the credits. There's also attending to be paid for, if you're shortlisted. If it's an international award, there are flights, hotels, delegate passes, food, drinks and so on. If it's local, can you stretch to a table so that you can celebrate with the entire project team and client? Remember, awards are only a cost if you don't win them. They're an investment if you do.

Is it good enough?

I'll use Cannes Lions 2024 as an example. In total, across all categories, there were 26,696 entries. Of those entries, 872 Lions were awarded. (Bear in mind that of those 872 Lions, most were silvers and bronzes, which are nice to have but don't have the new business or career cachet of a gold or Grand Prix.) This means that approximately only 1 in every 30 entries wins something. Or, for every £1,600 that is spent on a winning entry, £48,000 is spent on entries that don't win. Clearly, a lot of work is entered that isn't even close to being good enough. Having sat on countless juries over the years, I would estimate that more than half of the work entered stands no realistic chance of being considered for an award of any sort.

So, reduce the guesswork and the waste. Entering work that you think is good without assessing what you might be up against is a sure-fire way of becoming one of the 29 in every 30 entries that end up in the bin. Get realistic. Look at what has won over the last few years in the categories of the shows that you want to enter. This will give you a benchmark. Is your work really as good, if not better? Now look at how your work stacks up against the work that has been done globally and that will be in the same category as you. Still feeling confident? If you are, go for it. But if your work clearly isn't up to the same standards, or you think you might just be in with a squeak, save your money, or look for a less competitive local show if you really want to enter something.

If you've checked out the previous winners and this year's opposition and you're still optimistic, it's time to consider whether your case study and entries are as compelling as they could be. Show strangers, listen to the feedback, keep refining and building until the final whistle. Yes, it is a massive effort, but it's what the serial winners of awards do. And that is who you're up against. Take it seriously or save the money.

A realistic awards strategy.

Awards are worth the time, effort and cost of entering only if you win them. Now that you have an allocated budget and you've been through the process of confirming whether your work has a realistic chance, you need to work out a strategy for which awards to enter. Everyone who features at awards regularly has a clear strategy. They don't scatter-gun their approach; they target shows and categories.

I genuinely don't know how many advertising and design awards shows there are in the world. Awards-list.com suggests that there are at least 212. As ridiculous as that is, it does mean there is something for everyone, and your strategy doesn't have to revolve around the big festivals, such as Cannes Lions, D&AD and the One Show. Having said that, there's little point in entering an awards show that you or your clients have never heard of. It won't attract talent or business.

What are you looking to achieve? If you're making the best work in the world for the biggest and best brands, your strategy is pretty easy: go for the highest-profile awards out there to attract the most attention, talent and new business possible. If you aren't, or if you're doing amazing work that isn't international jury-friendly or is in a more niche space, find a more suitable awards. Think about the awards that you are more likely to win and target them. It's far better to dominate a respected smaller show than to be completely overlooked by a bigger one. At the very least, it will give you a decent PR story.

You could argue that if you aren't winning the big ones, why bother? I sympathise with that view, but there are countless great reasons to enter awards that don't require the awards to be a pencil or a lion. Consider why you're entering. Is it to give the team a boost, to have a great night out with a client, to celebrate and call out your skills in a more niche sector? Park the ego. Be realistic.

You need to understand **THE RULES OF THE GAME** around awards. It's a very practical thing. A lot of creative directors don't understand how to submit entries, know which shows to target or how to do a great case study.

Helen Andrews
CEO, Johannes Leonardo NY

It's not a level playing field.

Creativity is totally subjective, and all the judges have their own criteria for choosing winners. Juries are often heavily swayed by work from agencies or clients that are considered by common consensus to be fashionable that year. If you're not one of them, the mountain is just a little higher.

You also need to understand that the big international awards, such as Cannes, are dominated by the corporate communications groups. In 2024 some 80% of the shortlisted entries came from network agencies. They have developed something of a stranglehold because – quite understandably – they want awards that are recognised globally and can affect share prices. These awards also provide a brilliant platform for their global leadership teams to get together with senior clients from major brands and build relationships with a backdrop of creativity. Immense budgets are allocated by the groups to prepare work and case studies. Bragging rights and big accounts are at stake. The focus of Cannes is really to provide an arena for the groups to take on one another. The top CCOs in each group meet regularly to discuss how to improve the case studies and executions, and with them their chances of winning. Nothing is left to chance. And because the groups are by far the largest spenders, their senior employees make up most of the jury members, which provides them with the opportunity to lobby for work to be considered.

Now, if you work for one of those groups, that sounds like good news, right? It is. It's also the status quo and unlikely to change. However, if you're a small, independent agency, it's very hard to break in. At Cannes money talks. But if you have something genuinely brilliant, enter it regardless of what agency you're from. Don't let me put you off. It will win. And when it does, it will mean career-defining validation for you and your team. But if it isn't brilliant, consider putting your focus where the odds are a little more in your favour.

Share the love.

So you've won an award. Congratulations. You've defied the odds and shown the world what your creative leadership can deliver. You've posted on LinkedIn about being humbled and put it all over your agency socials. It's your moment in the sun. Hopefully, you've also used it to celebrate the entire team behind the project without bigging yourself up.

Giving credit to all the deserving members of the team who helped to create the work is a great way of saying that playing fair matters to you, and that you recognise and value everyone's contribution. You're demonstrating that you admire fairness as a behaviour and expect it in others. And, as we discussed in Chapter 8, the psychological safety this promotes will encourage everyone to perform to the best of their abilities. Grabbing the headlines for yourself or just the creatives is divisive and will damage any sense of team that you've built up. After all, why should anyone be expected to deliver their best efforts if they can't trust you to recognise them for it? You'll just force people to shout louder than each other in order to be seen. And that doesn't make a nice place to work. There's always enough credit to go around. Within reason, there are no limits on how many people can be recognised for contributing to awarded work. So be generous.

Your team will almost certainly have a few quiet, introverted members who never draw attention to themselves, regardless of how talented or pivotal they might be. For whatever reason, they don't care about taking credit and can easily get overlooked. Make sure they aren't. Go out of your way to celebrate their contribution. Taking the time to identify and reward the quiet stars who don't seek glory for themselves always generates goodwill across a business because it demonstrates integrity.

Morale and motivation.

No creative ever had the career ambition to work for a bunch of no-hopers. Everyone wants to believe that they're working somewhere capable of competing with the best agencies around. (Even if it's on only a few briefs a year.) They are looking to you not only to elevate the agency's creative ambitions, but also to validate their efforts and encourage them to feel proud of the work they're doing.

Never underestimate the power of your teams feeling proud of their work and of where they work. Simply entering awards is a tangible demonstration that you recognise their hard work and the quality of their thinking, and that you're prepared to spend money to show that you believe they are delivering to a high standard. It will also have a fantastic effect on the entire agency. Recognising the outstanding performance of a project team creates a sense of being part of something worthwhile, of belonging, while at the same time fostering a culture of excellence where everyone feels inspired to perform to higher levels in order to get the recognition they see being given to others. It's not only highly motivating, but also a great way to increase morale, job satisfaction and loyalty.

My only caveat is that this will succeed only if the work is genuinely good and everyone believes it is in with a chance. Otherwise, it's counterproductive or, worse, it makes you look as though your quality-control faculties are faulty. If the work is a step up for the business, but not quite up to awards standard, you might be better off giving out a team bonus or offering some career development training with the money you would have spent entering. But if you enter and win, happy days. It's incontrovertible proof that the business contains real talent and is going in the right direction, and that's the best boost to morale and motivation of all.

Judging.

I loved judging awards. It's like boot camp for creative direction. It offers a rare chance to engage properly with your peer group and hear their considered thoughts on what constitutes great creative work. Seeing work dissected forensically by the smartest minds in the business should be required learning for every creative. It was often reassuring to hear that their views were very similar to my own, but on the occasions that they weren't, it was an education to understand why. Judging awards can be time-consuming, but if you get the chance, take it. It is genuinely a good use of your time. You'll come out of it with renewed energy and determination to do better work, and a keener eye for what you need to do to produce winning work.

Judging is also a great networking event for creative leaders. In fact, it's one of the very few opportunities to compare experiences and knowledge, as there are no other organised forums to meet. Unlike other disciplines, we have no dedicated professional organisation to promote understanding of our professional skills. Consequently, being a creative leader can be very isolating, so it's liberating to be able to talk in a relaxed environment to a group of people who really understand at first hand the demands of the role.

The other benefit of judging is that it will boost your personal profile and that of your agency. Awards schemes publicise their jurors as a way of proving their credibility and attracting entries, and so they will always show you in a positive light as a respected industry leader. You can generally gauge the credibility of the award by who is judging it. But don't accept every offer. Tempting as it might be to have an expenses-paid trip somewhere lovely, it won't do your reputation any good to judge a dubious awards scheme.

See what you're up against.

For me, one of the best things about awards schemes has always been the opportunity to see the best work in the world, ranked by my peers, all in one place. I didn't always agree with the choices, but I always found it incredibly inspiring and instructive to see so many brilliant and innovative ideas. It never failed to make me more determined than ever to do better work. Sharing the winners of the main shows with the entire agency is a good way to remind them how competitive the industry is. Engage everyone in a conversation about the benefits of great work and fire them up to find new ways to produce it. It's no use just firing up the creative department – after all, they should be fired up to start with – you need everyone to want the same outcome and share the responsibility for making it happen.

Reviewing winning work also helped me to put the strengths and weaknesses of my own agency into context. Like it or not, awards shows are the best metric for gauging your strategic and creative resource capabilities. You are literally going head to head with your competitors. What are they doing that you are not? What do you need to change to be more competitive? Be sensible, though. If you're a small indie, don't beat yourself up because you haven't matched up to a global network agency; instead, compare yourself to your approximate competitive set. It's often an uncomfortable thing to do, but it's how potential clients and recruits are judging you, so you need to be aware of it.

Our industry is insanely competitive. Our successes and failures are all too public, and there's no escaping the relentless judgement of your work. If you want to succeed, you have no choice but to do better work than other people. And that's a lot easier when you know what the industry considers 'better' to look like.

There's a bit of advice I heard recently from a very successful football manager who has won the Champions League. He told me: 'LEARN FROM CHAMPIONS, not from players.' His view was that while all players perform, champions are the ones who have learned how to face the greatest challenges, pressures and standards and still come out on top. It means that even when they fail, they learn from it and do something about it.

Rob Campbell
CSO, Colenso NZ

I'm a big believer in awards for the right reasons. I GET REALLY WORRIED though when I see someone who's highly awarded and I've never heard of anything they've done.

Rob Campbell
CSO, Colenso NZ

Scam.

Yes, it happens. Yes, it is virtually institutionalised in some businesses. And yes, it gives advertising, communications, design and anyone who does it, or does nothing to stop it, a bad name. Fortunately it's not as widespread as the rumours suggest, and certainly not among the most awarded work. Winning big with scam ads is really tough thanks to platforms like LinkedIn, where scams are regularly called out. To have your work publicly humiliated or your award rescinded is also incredibly damaging to the reputation of a client or agency, and fewer people are now willing to sanction the risk of getting caught.

There are different levels of scam, though, and one person's definition might not be the same as another's. There's scam that is work created specifically for awards for which someone has managed to find a small, relevant client. That is typically a brand that couldn't possibly afford to hire a big ad agency under normal circumstances – a local barber or a small charity, perhaps – which only has to agree to stick its logo on the work to get it all for free. There's scam that is work that a bigger client, often a retained account, has let the agency make at its own cost. There's scam that is amended from the version that ran. There's scam that involves the doctoring of the case-study problem and outcomes. And so on. It's all scam. The only work that should be entered is real work to a real brief, paid for by a client whose business it has had a demonstrable impact on.

No agency or client will ever admit to scamming. Every awards scheme will tell you that it is a tiny issue and almost never happens. But it does, and we all know it does. All industries are subject to fraud in some form or another, and I suppose as far as frauds go this isn't the end of the world. Unfortunately, it does nothing to reassure clients that we are smart, hard-working partners for them. If you see it, call it out. Public pressure is the only way it will stop.

Notes.

Notes.

Notes.

Index.

A

account management department 88–9
active listening 128
adapting to change 194–211
advertising, death of 211
agencies: agency partners 91
   agency positioning 41
   awards 217, 222, 226
   culture 50
   gang culture 171
   resource percentages 180
AI (artificial intelligence) 46, 195, 210
Andrews, Helen 15, 113, 185, 221
Angelou, Maya 151
appraisals 108
arguments 27, 163
Atkin, Lynsey 15, 61, 169, 215
awards 46, 212–29

B

Beale, Claire 15
Beresford-Hill, Chris 15, 25, 105, 113
bills, paying 187
Birkbeck College 143
bonuses 49, 102, 187
brain 55, 65, 71, 156, 166, 204
brands, image 47
briefs: choosing 24
   directing creative departments 101
   financial implications 184
   production budgets 192
Brim, Richard 15, 52, 67, 103, 148, 197
budgets *see* finances
'builds only' policy 164
burnout 65, 209

C

Campbell, Rob 15, 80, 170, 227–8
Cannes Lions 8, 219, 220, 222
case studies 81, 137–8, 201, 207, 217, 218, 229

cash reserves 187
celebrate the work 110
CEO (Chief Executive Officer) 78, 179, 189
CFO (Chief Financial Officer) 179, 189
change: adapting to 194–211
   fear of 204
   resistance to 209
chaos 55–73, 160
Chesters, Kevin 15, 51, 77, 122, 216
clients: agency positioning 41
   and awards 217
   client relationships 45
   expectations 90
   long-term clients 191
   new business leads 44
   pitches 136–53
   production budgets 192
   relationship with 116–135
   updates 124
CMO (Chief Marketing Officer) 45
coaches 72
cognitive diversity 166
Coleman, Harvey 47
collaborative creativity 159
commercials of creativity 170–93
communication 35
   appraisals 108
   and expectations 75–6
   pitches 143, 149–51
   problems and 164
   producers 43
   right-hand people 60
   updating clients 124
confidence: account management 88
   appraisals 108
   'builds only' policy 164
   and change 196
   clients and 118, 133
   decision-making 27
   delegation 63
   lack of 98

leadership 96, 149, 168
   Messenger Effect 127
   pitches 150
   psychological safety 163
   reviews 107
   self-confidence 26
conflict 27, 53, 163
confrontation 27, 163
consistency 31
control freaks 64
coping strategies 32
CPO (Chief Production Officer) 82, 179
creative coaches 72
creative culture 154–73
creative department: building and running 94–115
   expectations 85
   pruning 112
creative space 114–15
creativity: definition 155–6
   finances of 174–93
   training 173
credit, giving 168, 169, 223
criticism 111, 153
critique, creative culture 164
CSO (Chief Strategic Officer) 81, 87, 145, 179
culture 50
curiosity 173, 176
cynicism 198, 199

D

D&AD 220
death of advertising 211
decision-making: clients 120
   confidence 27
delegation 59–63
department budgets 189
direction, creative departments 101
disabled employees 49
diversity, hiring creatives 104, 166
Droga, David 186
Dungate, Scott 15, 69, 89, 165, 186

E

emotional awareness 53
emotional intelligence 23
empathy 23, 31, 204
employee retention 49
enemies, gang culture 171

environment 172
exec coaches 72
executions: brand strategy 31
   writing pitches 146
expectations 74–93, 127, 129
expenses 187
experts, adapting to change 208
exposure 47

F

FD (Financial Director) 179
fear, overcoming 204
feedback: from clients 130–1
   pitches 153
   psychological safety 163
filmmaking 130
finances 175–93
   and awards 218, 219
   cash flow 187
   cost of pitches 191
   departmental budgets 189
   expenses 187
   headhunters 193
   production budgets 192
   project creep 184
   resource percentages 180
   resource scoping 182–3
   time sheets 188
firing creatives 112
fixed costs 191

G

gang culture 171
Gatsky Sinclair, Charlie 15, 83, 109, 162, 205
Gen Z 210
global CCO (Chief Creative Officer) 86
goals 92
Google 163
Grieve, Alex 15, 26, 33, 70, 97, 100, 147

H

happiness 21
headhunters 108, 193, 217
Hegarty, John 186
help, asking for 66–7
Hemming, Bronwen 15, 181
high standards 30
hiring creatives 102, 104–5, 112, 166, 193
hobbies 71, 123

holidays 71
homework, pitches 142, 150
HOPM (Head of Project Management) 42
Hulley, Nicholas 15, 62, 84, 126
hybrid working 115

I

idiots 167
IKEA Effect 101
image 47
imposter syndrome 92-3
industry PR 46
insecurity 53, 140
Instagram 46
internet 198
interns 102
introverts 35, 150, 223

JK

jealousy 53
job satisfaction 210
job security 108
judging awards 225
junior clients 133
juries, awards 222
knowledge 201

L

leadership: agency culture 50
  and creative departments 94-115
  delegation 59-63
  expectations of 74-93
  inspiring others 22
  letting go 64
  nurturing creatives 28
  pastoral care 49
  team management 40
learning new skills 68-9, 201, 210
Leonard, Nils 186
letting go 64
LinkedIn 46, 223, 229
listening to clients 128
lists, to-do 73
Livesey, Tanya 15, 34, 47, 135
looking after yourself 71
Lossgott, Nadja 15, 57, 161
loyalty, gang culture 171

M

Mackay-Sinclair, Katie 15, 29, 79, 99, 121, 151, 157, 177
MD (Managing Director) 179
memorability, pitches 152
mental health 173
mentors 72, 109, 133, 140
Messenger Effect 127
mini-me syndrome 104-5
morale 224
motivation 224

N

network agencies 222
networking 91, 225
new business 44, 191, 217
nurturing ideas 28

O

office politics 53
offices 114-15, 172
Ogilvy, David 180
One Show 220
open-plan offices 115
optimism 198, 202
over-delivering 129

PQ

pastoral care 49
pay rises 102
percentages, resource 180
performance 47
Pie, Theory of 47
pitches 148-65, 191
planning: coping with chaos 59
  pitches 141, 150
  time off 71
  to-do lists 73
planning department 87, 115
PM (project manager) 42
politics 53
positives, focusing on 203
power: knowledge as 201
  responsibility and 98
praise 110
preparation 38
  pitches 142, 150
presentation, pitches 143, 150-1
pressure, coping with 22

pride, gang culture 171
problem-solving 31
'Problem Spotters' 141
production 43
production budgets 192
productivity 172, 173
profits 183–85
Project Aristotle 163
project creep 184
project management 42, 88
psychological safety 163, 223
public relationships, industry PR 46
questions, pitches 153

R

references, hiring creatives 102
rehearsals, pitches 143, 149, 151
relentlessness 32
resource percentages 180
resource scoping 182, 183
responsibility 24, 28, 37, 98
retention rates 210
reviews 42, 107
Richter, Felix 15, 93, 106, 131
right-hand people 60–3
Rudd, Charlie 15, 125, 190
rules, and creative culture 159, 160
Russell, Bertrand 87

S

safety, psychological 163, 223
scam ads 217, 229
Scott, Bill 15, 39, 48, 158, 200, 206
self-awareness 23, 50, 53, 75
shoots 130
skills, upskilling 210
sleep 65
Sobral, Rodrigo 15, 58, 119, 199
Spencer, David 15, 144, 178, 182
standards, high 30
strategies: awards 220
   consistency 31
stress 107, 111, 172
Syed, Matthew 104, 166
symbols, gang culture 171

T

talent acquisition 193
task forces, adapting to change 207, 208

team management: appraisals 108
   creative departments 94–115
   department budgets 189
   giving credit to 168, 169, 223
   leadership 40
   morale and motivation 224
   pitches 141, 145
   psychological safety 163, 223
   reviews 40, 107
   right-hand people 60–3
temperament 22
Thatcher, Margaret 98
Theory of Pie 47
thinking time 65
time, and awards 218
time off 71
time sheets 188
to-do lists 73
training 68–9
   creativity training 173
   employee retention 49
   knowledge as power 201
   rehearsals 151
   upskilling 210
turnover 187

UVW

under-promising 129
updating clients 124
upskilling 210
weaknesses, identifying 66–7, 68, 76
win ratios 191
Wired 198
work/life balance 49, 71
work-shy creatives 112
working class, hiring creatives 104
working hours 70
World Economic Forum 155
writing pitches 143, 146

MICK MAHONEY has more than thirty years' experience at the very top of UK advertising.

He is one of the most awarded creatives of his generation, including the coveted Cannes Grand Prix and The One Show Best in Show, as well as multiple Lions, Pencils and Arrows. He has also been a member of the Cannes Lions Film Jury and the D&AD Black Pencil Jury, and Chairman of the D&AD film jury.

Mick has been placed on the definitive *Campaign* magazine's Top UK CD list at each of the three agencies he was the CCO of, an achievement unsurpassed in the UK.

As a creative director he has run some of the most famous brands in the world, including Johnnie Walker, British Airways, The BBC, Vodafone and Amnesty International, among many others.

He is also co-author of the best-selling book *The Creative Nudge*, published by Laurence King.

Mick is now focused on using his extensive experience and knowledge of creativity and the creative industries as a full-time Creative Coach and Consultant to individuals, agencies and brands.

If you would like to know more about Mick, go to: mcreativeindustries.com